The Ninth Decade

The Ninth Decade

An Octogenarian's Chronicle

Carl H. Klaus

University of Iowa Press ❧ Iowa City

University of Iowa Press, Iowa City 52242
Copyright © 2021 by Carl H. Klaus
www.uipress.uiowa.edu
Printed in the United States of America
Design by Sara T. Sauers
Printed on acid-free paper

Library of Congress Cataloging-in-Publication Data
Names: Klaus, Carl H., author.
Title: The Ninth Decade: An Octogenarian's Chronicle /
    by Carl Hanna Klaus.
Description: Iowa City: University of Iowa Press, [2021] |
    Includes index. | Identifiers: LCCN 2021001152 (print) |
    LCCN 2021001153 (ebook) |
    ISBN 9781609387860 (paperback; acid-free paper) |
    ISBN 9781609387877 (ebook)
Subjects: LCSH: Klaus, Carl H. | Aging. | Older people—
    Conduct of life. | Old age—Psychological aspects. |
    English teachers—Iowa—Biography.
Classification: LCC HQ1061.K54 2021 (print) | LCC HQ1061 (ebook) |
    DDC 305.26/1 [B—dc23
LC record available at https://lccn.loc.gov/2021001152
LC ebook record available at https://lccn.loc.gov/2021001153

To Jackie,
Heroine and Muse

Contents 身

Preface 🌿

THIS WORK IS a product of good luck and irrepressible curiosity that arrived on my eightieth birthday, eight and a half years ago. I wanted to know about life after eighty, but could find no specialized or personal books on the subject. Uncharted territory, so I decided to chronicle my eighties, also noting the experiences of other octogenarians—loved ones, friends, acquaintances—and thereby produce a collective depiction of life after eighty.

Unlike daily entries in a journal, the essays in this work encompass six-month periods, from my early eighties to late eighties, each essay based on notes that I made throughout the period. For each time period, I have noted a few telegraphic subtitles that suggest the widely varied matters that most concerned me during that time, as in "Eighty-Four: Decrepitude, Wisdom, Shingles, Downsizing."

Collectively the subtitles reflect challenges and pleasures I experienced during this late life marathon.

November 26, 2020

The Ninth Decade

Eighty and Before ⫣

Longevity, Leisure, Aging without Aging

FEBRUARY 2013

I'm eighty going on eighty-one this coming May. Getting on in years, but I often feel as I did in my seventies, and look almost like I did back then. More surprising, I might live into the mid nineties, according to Patti, the captivating nurse who oversees the cardiac rehab where I work out on the treadmill four or five days a week. She made that astonishing conjecture when I was planning this chronicle, focused on my experience of aging. Which led me to wonder how many years I might be around to work on it. That's when Patti projected a lifespan in the mid nineties. "But just to be on the safe side," she said, "you'd best confine it to your eighties."

Eighty-year-olds, I was surprised to learn, are the fastest-growing demographic throughout the industrialized world. In the United States, there are more than nine million octogenarians (about one out of ten persons), and the number will rise to over fifteen million by 2025. But gerontologists have not done longitudinal studies of octogenarian life. And octogenarians themselves have written so little about their eighties—a couple of one-year journals published more than twenty years ago—that the ninth decade, an exceptional period of life, is uncharted territory. To shed some light on it, I intend to produce a multi-year account of my eighties, taking into account the experience of friends and family members also in their eighties.

As for life in one's nineties, I'll leave that story to Jackie, my loving partner, who might outlast me by ten or fifteen years, thanks to her stellar condition. How else to describe the condition of someone who takes no prescribed medicine and suffers from none of the usual afflictions of aging, except for a lazy gut and a one-hour bladder? Whereas I have a sluggish thyroid, enlarged prostate, chronic kidney disease, coronary artery disease, cataracts in both eyes, hearing aids in both ears, itching on both arms and legs, Raynaud's syndrome in both hands, and can't rise to the occasion without a dose of Viagra. And that's just a partial list of my so-called "health issues" at the University of Iowa Hospitals and Clinics. Jackie, I should add, had breast cancer several years ago and got through it with verve, as if it weren't a health issue at all. I, on the other hand, could hardly force a grin during my bout with Hodgkin's lymphoma a couple of years ago.

More to the point, Jackie's still working full time as a realtor, whereas I retired from the University of Iowa sixteen years ago. And she remembers most of her clients from the past forty years, despite a mild stroke a few years before we met, while I've forgotten most of the students who populated my classrooms. It's not just her memory that impresses me. It's also her exercise routine, for while I need twenty minutes on the treadmill to reach my maximum speed of 3.2 miles an hour with a seven percent incline, she starts out at four miles an hour and in five minutes reaches her maximum of six miles an hour with a seven percent incline. And that's just her warm-up for fifty more minutes of other exercises—lunges, squats, sit-ups, and the like. A working mind in a working body, driven by the demands of her real estate business. So, we live apart during the week in our separate homes and come together on the weekends at my place, where she keeps in touch with her clients on a smartphone and iPad while I'm still using a dumbphone and laptop.

The only work I've been doing lately is to make my way through the annual seed catalogs, looking for new varieties to try out in my vegetable garden, then taking stock of my viable seeds from previous years, then planning what to grow in each of the seasons, and finally ordering seeds, row covers, and the like. A late winter ritual I performed for so many years it once seemed as inevitable as the rotation of the seasons, until two years ago when Hodgkin's lymphoma and chemo meant that a garden was out of the question, so the catalog ritual was also out of the question, which led me to wonder what else would be out of the question. A few months later, when I was in the later stage of chemo, my upbeat oncologist regaled me with the news that he didn't see any reason why I couldn't live to be ninety-nine, which made me wonder why he didn't say one hundred. But no sooner was I in remission than he urged me to "do something special, like a trip abroad sometime during the coming months"—not, as it turned out, in celebration, but in recognition that there's a fifty percent chance of recurrence during the first year in remission, which made me wonder what had happened to my chances of reaching ninety-nine. On the other hand, now that I've been in remission some twenty months, the odds have surely improved so much I might have a good chance of reaching one hundred or more.

How strange that I'm only a few paragraphs into this piece and my thoughts keep circling around the question of how long I might live, whereas longevity rarely crossed my mind until I was beset by lymphoma and then started work on this project. Probably a result of the articles I've been reading in the *New York Times* "New Old Age" blog, getting up to speed on the subject. Thus far I've only read several months of the blog, but it often focuses on the circumstances of people so advanced in age or compromised in health as to need special care of one kind or another. "Assisted living" it's called—a euphemism that resonates with a host of medical, psychological, social, financial, and legal issues. Thus, the question of longevity is unavoidable, as in any discussion of aging or old-age planning. Now that the question keeps coming to mind, I wonder what it would be like to have Jackie's stamina and bill of health, to be as fit as she—and have a good chance of living into my nineties or beyond—without any need of assisted living. And therefore without any need to give up the home I've lived in and the gardens I've tended the past forty-three years.

But it's also clear that my four-story house on a three-quarter-acre lot is not a good long-term fit for an eighty-year-old, especially since my garden helper is graduating from the university this spring and the cleaning lady just told me it's too much for her aging body. Which makes me wonder if it might soon be too much for mine as well. It's certainly not as suitable as Jackie's little house on a postage stamp lot—her place so elegant and immaculate it looks like a still life, everything arranged just so, whereas mine looks so much like real life that she's often urging me to declutter the attic, the cellar, and everything in between before I shuffle off this mortal coil. All of which is to say she's as organized as an elementary school teacher, and I'm as in need of discipline as one of her former third-graders, romping up and down the place as if my sun might never set.

Cluttered though they are, those multiple floors help keep me in shape, as does the uphill-downhill backyard. And the neighborhood keeps me in touch with a run of life that seems like life itself—college students on one side, middle-aged working parents with teenagers on the other, an octogenarian couple behind me, a few single women in separate houses across the street, and a small nursery school nearby. A range of life I'm not yet ready to trade for the ease of a retirement home. Seventy-five years ago, such places were a rarity, as I recall from my childhood, for old folks back then often lived with their children and grandchildren. The extended family was still intact, coexisting under a single roof, enriching the lives of everyone in the family. Now, of course, retirement homes proliferate like morning mushrooms. But now, as I discovered from the government's statistics on aging, millions of aged people are not only living apart from their children and grandchildren, but also outside of retirement homes, so I'm evidently not alone on that score.

And I'm probably not alone in wondering what living into my nineties might be like, especially given the increasing number of eighty-year-olds in the government's statistics. But I can't imagine what I might make of those additional years to deserve such a gift of time, when already it seems I'm a lotus-eater. Nothing on my docket but whatever I happen to be writing at the moment and whatever manuscript I'm reading for a series of nonfiction books I coedit for Iowa's university press.

How can I justify this extended life, when aside from reading, writing, editing, and occasional trips to picturesque places with Jackie, it's dominated by the pleasures of gardening, cooking, and savoring delectable dishes that I contrive or come upon in newspapers and magazines. Like the classic sautée of large shrimp, also known as scampi, that involves only a few ingredients, perfectly matched as if they were meant for one another, especially when quickly cooked in an order that perfectly marries them. First some melted butter waiting to release the seductive aroma of minced garlic, enhanced by the addition of some dry white wine, salt, and pepper, yielding a tangy bath for the shrimp, brightened after a few minutes by lemon juice, and topped off with minced parsley. A deliciously easy ten- to fifteen-minute prep, well matched with thin spaghetti or a baguette of French bread.

Having turned into a self-indulgent gastronome, I wonder what other eighty-year-olds do with their leisure time and what they think of their doings. Questions that came to mind a few weeks ago when Jackie and I were in California visiting my brother and sister-in-law at a pricey retirement complex in Palo Alto, and then our Iowa City friends Dick and Phyllis who winter in Rancho Mirage—a fittingly named adjunct of Palm Springs. I didn't want to dispel the mirage by asking them to reflect on their leisurely existence, so I smiled my way through the visits. I've recently been thinking about my leisurely doings, thanks to a call from my daughter Hannah, an artist, art therapist, and grief counselor, who works at the University of California Children's Hospital in Sacramento caring for seriously ill children.

Now in her late fifties, Hannah told me of being concerned with what her life adds up to and then asked how things look from my perspective. Which led me to tell her "you do so much for so many people, you have nothing to worry about when it comes to taking stock of yourself." Compared to Hannah, who's a prolific painter and collagist, I feel like a slacker with nothing but a book or essay or recipe in progress. An unsettling thought that makes me wonder what matters in the course of a life, especially since my books could never make such a difference in the lives of others as Hannah's art therapy makes every day in the lives of those suffering children.

Given their afflictions, it seems like a luxury to be writing about the ins and outs of aging, rather than doing something closer to the bone and more purposeful in the time that's left. Like the vividly detailed cancer blog that my former student Susan has been writing for the *New York Times.* The fate of loved ones, friends, and former students like Susan also makes me wonder about the worth of these musings. Especially when I think of my wife Kate, swept away ten years ago by a cerebral hemorrhage. Or my friend Skip, whom I'd known for sixty years, undone by cancer last month despite being healthy enough to fly here two years ago and visit me in the hospital after giving a piano recital at the university. But how else can I honor them if not by taking account of their destinies and my own, by heeding John Donne's conviction that "no man is an island entire of itself; every man is a piece of the continent, a part of the main."

No sooner do I feel the urgency of those resonant words than something deep within me rebels, refusing its tacit imperative to do something consequential every day of my remaining existence, as if life were a morality play and nothing but incessant and high-minded productivity could justify one's being. Must be some puritanical strain coming out in those last few sentences, the presence of which makes me want to run in the opposite direction, shouting for joy in the freedom of my years. Seizing the day. Exulting as I did in Venice last fall, especially one night by the Grand Canal, aglow with Soave, imagining Jackie and I might never leave, that our candle might never burn down. Maybe that's what I should have said to Hannah, but I assume she'll read it right here in this paragraph and in *A Self Made of Words*, the little book now in press that I wrote while recovering from cancer. Now that the lymphoma is in remission and I'm scheduled for cataract surgery next month, the only problem that really bothers me is my profound hearing loss.

I started to lose it in my early fifties, unable sometimes to decipher all the words of a soft-spoken student, or to hear what Kate was saying when I was on the third floor and she on the second. I probably did myself in by mowing our lawn for fifteen years without noise-reduction earmuffs and long before that by playing a homemade hi-fi rig at high volume in my one-room college apartment. While my hearing problem early on was mild enough to be remedied by a tiny pair of aids in the ear canal, it's now so much worse that I need over-the-ear digital aids with special programs to cope with speech in noise or in wind or on telephones. Yet even with those high-tech aids, I'm hapless whenever the give-and-take is too quick or too dense, or there's too much background noise. An impairment so extreme, I'm dismayed by how many things are now out of reach, like vocal concerts and stage productions. Movies are only intelligible with captions or caption readers. Even conversation is problematic unless I'm face-to-face with one person who talks at a moderate pace and whose pronunciation and voice are clear and strong, like those of graduate students and faculty at the university's audiology clinic. Sitting across the table from Jackie at lunch or dinner, I sometimes miss a crucial word, given the softness of her voice or the competing sound of my own chewing, which leaves both of us frustrated—or amused, if my misunderstanding is sufficiently comic.

Aside from deficient hearing, I often feel so good it's difficult to believe I'm afflicted with all the health issues I noted a few pages back, a paradox that makes me wonder how one can have such insidious conditions without being undone by them. More to the point, I don't have aches and pains in my knees or hips, and I don't feel as if my mind is losing its way. Nor have I fallen the past year, though doctors and nurses continue to ask that question, as if anyone with white hair were at risk of losing her balance. Perhaps I'm experiencing what lifespan theorists and gerontologists refer to as the "new longevity," by which they evidently mean old age without the usual debilities of advanced age. In other words, aging without aging.

There's no such thing, of course, but that's the fantasy hovering around the edge of such phrases as "new longevity" or "new old age." Never mind the patent contradiction of terms. "New" is the dream word, the glittering promise that offsets "old," that comes to the rescue of bodily decrepitude, embodying an almost irresistible suggestion that aging can be arrested or possibly even reversed. Indeed, that's what will soon happen to me in part, thanks to the new intraocular lenses I'll get during cataract surgery next month, enabling me to see as well as I did some forty years ago. And if need be there are also new hip joints and new kneecaps to match the other new parts that medical engineers have fabricated to keep us going beyond our years, like the stents in my coronary arteries that keep the pathways open so the blood keeps flowing and my heart keeps beating. No wonder my aged friends talk about their health issues and the new medical treatments that might cure them. Or even more audacious new ways of dealing with the infirmities of age, as when a recent bout of fatigue led Jackie to tell me "the end game . . . means figuring out new ways to play this part of life."

When I was younger, it never occurred to me to think of old age as if it were a chess match and one could checkmate the grim reaper. But that's the unspoken dream, the magical thinking inherent in "figuring out new ways to play this part of life." Which reminds me of a time in the latter years of my childhood when I imagined that I would never die, as my parents had a few years before. And now given the good fortune of recovering swiftly from stage 4 lymphoma, I sometimes catch myself again feeling almost invulnerable. Or at least supposing, as I once did, that diet, exercise, timely medical care, and stress-free living can keep one going and going and going. But neither the diet nor the tranquility, nor exercise nor excellent medical care prevented Kate's sudden demise. Ever since then, I've been inclined to think that longevity is determined as much by fate or luck or chance or whatever one chooses to call it, like the unusual bit of good luck that enabled me to survive my second heart attack.

It took place seven years ago in Red Wing, Minnesota, fifty miles from the Mayo Clinic in Rochester. An ambulance from the local hospital whizzed me to Mayo in less than an hour, while Jackie followed in my Jeep. A few days later, after stents were installed in two arteries, we were on our way home, thanks to much less traumatic surgery than the bypass after my first heart attack, twenty-one years before. If the heart attack had taken place 350 miles north of the clinic, in the remote cabin overlooking Lake Superior where Jackie and I had been staying just two days before, an ambulance might not have been fast enough for me to get life-saving care, so I'm fortunate the attack took place in Red Wing.

Speaking of good fortune, of life-saving good fortune, a little more than two years ago Jackie and I went out to dinner at a local restaurant and there encountered my former cardiologist, Allyn, whom I hadn't seen since he retired a few years before. He asked how I was doing, but rather than telling him anything about my heart, I belabored him with an account of the disturbing conditions that had been afflicting me for several months—extreme fatigue, night sweats, anemia, and relentless itching all over my body, which my local internist had diagnosed as byproducts of an iron deficiency and an allergy. Allyn, however, gave me the name of two oncologists at the university's cancer clinic and urged me to call one the next day for an appointment, which led to a diagnosis of stage 4 Hodgkin's lymphoma. A life-saving diagnosis, thanks to the coincidence of that evening's encounter.

Now that I think of it, that story, like the other, reflects the dependence of my long life on the marvels of contemporary medicine: the stents that enabled me to survive my second heart attack, and the special chemo that got me through cancer. Or should I chalk up those survivals to the good fortune of living at a time when such treatments are available? Had I suffered those problems twenty-five years earlier, before the existence of those remedies, I'd surely not have lived to be eighty, feeling well enough to write about it. A spur to keep working on this chronicle.

Eighty to Eighty-One ✒

Health Care, Exercise, Estrangement

Three cheers for cataract surgery! Thanks to new artificial lenses, I can read without a magnifying glass, compute without zooming in, and drive at night without the blinding glare of oncoming headlights. A recovery that still seems remarkable, given the painlessness and brevity of each operation (twenty minutes on my left eye in early March and twenty on my right eye in late March), surgeries that have enabled me to see things as clearly and vividly as when I was in my early forties.

A day after the second surgery, I stopped at the co-op for a few groceries and told all the clerks of my good fortune, which led Juli the cashier to exclaim, "You just had it done?" "Yesterday morning," said I, my enthusiasm irrepressible, to which she responded by telling me about her father, a retired farmer, whose refusal to have cataract surgery has diminished the quality of his life. Her sad tale made me feel a sense of remorse for having blurted out my good news, and then a hunger to make it right by urging Juli to dispel his resistance with a report of my experience. But she, being of good humor and wise in the ways of her father, put me at ease with the fact of his obstinacy—a reminder that aging is a deeply personal matter, influenced by habits of mind and patterns of a lifetime, so its effects cannot always be remedied by the wonders of medical science. And sometimes the aging of others leaves one at a loss that nothing can alter, as I discovered when Patti, the head nurse at cardiac rehab, retired in late March. She had not only helped me plan the scope of this journal but also guided me through seven years of exercise following my second heart attack, so it's not surprising that I was saddened by her retirement. In the days and weeks after Patti left, I missed her more than I had expected—missed her infectious laugh and lively sense of humor, as well as her empathy and all-around medical know-how. Now I realize she had become such a caring presence in my life that it was difficult to accept her departure. But I don't want to sound like a forlorn admirer, since I might well be considered a fickle patient, having fallen for another Patti just a month after Patti retired.

Talk about the madcap behavior of age! I met the new Patti, a masterful nurse practitioner, in early May at the survivor's clinic of the university cancer center, where she gave me a thorough checkup, poking and probing and questioning me (a surveillance, she called it in her report). I'm pleased not only that the lymphoma is still in remission but also that she didn't discover any new issues, and that the blood test showed my kidney function slightly improved. Given advanced chronic kidney disease, the ability of my kidneys to filter poison out of my blood is severely reduced and additional declines in kidney function would require dialysis (artificial filtration of the blood) in order to survive. No wonder her news of their slight improvement was like a gift, especially since her report arrived in the mail on my birthday. Maybe my admiration for the new Patti was simply a result of her painstaking attention to my case, which makes me hope she stays on my case.

But I wish there weren't so many on my case that it seems like I'm on a medical merry-go-round. Taking my pulse so often I've become all too conscious of it and all the other markers of my bodily condition, such as blood tests, urine tests, and CT scans. Which makes me wonder if my expanding network of specialists is a feature of the new old age—survival via perpetual medical observation. Yet it was fascinating to be examined in late July by my cardiologist, who not only went through the usual business of listening to my heart and lungs, but also made a point of telling me about a new research report, something he's never done before, indicating that persons on statins, as I've been for some fifteen years, have a reduced incidence of dementia. His typically low-key manner suddenly gave way to a broad smile as he told me, "It's good news for all of us." In all my appointments with him, I cannot recall seeing such expansive delight on his face, his professional persona briefly falling away to reveal the aged person himself, an octogenarian animated by the same hopes and fears as my own, in this case the dread we all have of something worse than mortality—the living death of dementia.

I remember my first encounter with it in the person of my Aunt Celia, who mothered me for several years after the death of my mother, reduced in her late sixties to plucking at the hem of her skirt, muttering "der, die, das, den, der, die, das, den," rehearsing Germanic forms of the definite article she must have memorized many years before. Which made me wonder if dementia is in my genes too. Sometimes I dismiss the thought by noting that I'm now more than ten years older than she was back then, and I've long since abandoned, though I once craved, the German-Hungarian high-cholesterol cuisine of which she was a master. I've also just finished the Sunday New York Times crossword puzzle for the fourth consecutive week, which leads me to think dementia is not in my future. But Aunt Celia probably never imagined it in hers, either.

Dementia is such a widely known byproduct of aging that I was puzzled by the New York Times publication of two lengthy articles on consecutive days this month, each about a nonagenarian with dementia, one a legendary sports statistician, the other a "memory lady" who once knew hundreds of books by heart and recited them for women's clubs. Unusual cases of late age memory loss? Or cautionary notes from the Times to anyone craving an exceptionally long life?

But enough of these gloomy reflections. Better to celebrate the pre-breakfast running routine of my son, Marshall, who does a few miles every morning. When he called today and I asked if he's been able to keep it up in the heat and humidity of Little Rock, his answer took me by surprise: "In a week or so, dad, I'll gradually start working up to eight or nine miles a day, to get ready for a half marathon this fall." At his age, fifty-five, I couldn't have run a single mile, though I walked down and back from campus every day, a total of three miles. Indeed, when I was fifty-three, shortly after my first heart attack and triple bypass, my cardiologist urged me not to run: "It won't do you any more good than walking, and it'll save your knees in the long run." But Marshall is certainly more fit and muscular than I ever was, which makes me think he'll age far better than I. What a difference between his generation and mine. We had calisthenics in school but nothing like the current devotion to daily physical exercise and strenuous challenges.

Like an echo of Marshall's challenging activity, my colleague Ruedi surprised me a few hours later at a birthday dinner for his seventy-first with the news he had returned the day before from RAGBRAI, *The Des Moines Register*'s Annual Great Bike Ride across Iowa. This year, from Council Bluffs on the Missouri River to Fort Madison on the Mississippi, a total of 440 miles in seven days. A formidable task for any age, especially for someone Ruedi's age. And he did it on a one-speed bike of 1904 vintage, like the one he used when he was in the Swiss Army Bicycling Corps. The best part of Ruedi's story was his report that "I felt stronger than ever on the third day of the ride," as if the ride itself, which had evidently taxed him the first two days, enabled him to transcend his age in the midst of it. I wonder if it had something to do with the steep elevations of the first two days compared to the less steep inclines of the third. Whatever the case, Ruedi is a model of fitness and a demon for athletic challenges—come September he's going on a 1500-mile biking adventure from Astoria, Oregon, to Newport Beach, California. I wonder how much stronger he'll feel at the end of that bike ride. Maybe the secret of aging is in the challenges we confront.

The more we take on, the stronger we become.

I was thinking that might be the case early this month after a day in my large vegetable bed, weeding its 44' × 22' border, pulling out a failed row of cauliflower plants, harvesting beans, zucchini, and cherry tomatoes, transplanting chard seedlings for a fall crop, and tilling some open patches of ground with my one-wheel plow to ready things for seeding in beets, radishes, and turnips. So much up and down, back and forth, and crawling around, it left me feeling like the Tin Woodman, my hips and knees stiff and sore even though I took intermittent fifteen- to thirty-minute breaks throughout the day to ease the stress. But the next morning I arose without any pain at all, much as Ruedi felt stronger after the uphill biking on RAGBRAI.

Later that morning, I encountered my friend Hank and was surprised to see a tennis racket in the front seat of his car, even though he was sitting there with a brace on his left knee. "Some people never learn," said I, surprised that an eighty-three-year-old would be out on the court after having knee replacement surgery a few months ago. "I'm only playing twice a week, and I plan to slack off a bit, but if you don't push your body and push it hard, you'll lose it. It's as simple as that." So, I keep pushing my body in the garden and at the cardiac rehab.

When it comes to pushing oneself in the face of challenges, I think my fifty-four-year-old daughter Amy might win a prize, for she's beset with lupus, celiac disease, and other auto-immune conditions yet continues to work full time, sometimes overtime, as a registered nurse. And she does so without complaint, sending me buoyant emails with shots of flowers along her walks. I think she must be playing mind games with herself. How else to overcome the incurable fatigue of lupus? Whenever I'm troubled by incurable conditions, I too play mind games with myself. I also keep pushing my mind with the *Sunday Times* crossword puzzle, this ongoing chronicle, and the manuscripts I review for the nonfiction series that I edit.

But the reading, writing, and puzzling haven't done anything to improve my memory, for I'm often stumped by the name of a person or the title of a book or the details of an incident I should know without a moment's hesitation. A few days ago, I went to buy a couple of books but drew a blank when asked what I was looking for. Later that afternoon, Jackie asked me to drive by a house she had just sold that I didn't remember having seen before, which led to a surprised query: "Don't you remember the Christmas cocktail parties there and how difficult it was to find a parking space, so we had to walk two or three blocks each time in the cold wind?" I didn't remember anything of the sort—neither the house, the parties, the difficulty parking, the cold wind, nor the hostess's red hair. And I was momentarily dismayed not only by that lapse but by all the others that had elicited her frequent query, "Don't you remember?" Yet the memory of all those lapses is itself a consolation that I haven't completely lost my power of recollection. How's that for mind games?

It's not just my memory that's in trouble, for I discovered during the past year on the university press's editorial board that I'm so out of touch with current research in my academic fields that I felt unfit for the task and resigned from it earlier this month. A strange experience, since I've never resigned from anything before, considering it a matter of professional integrity to fulfill such obligations. But I'm also aware of not having kept up to date with things, whereas my recently retired colleague David, who's also on the board, evidently has no trouble. A sign of aging that's difficult to ignore and painful to recognize, as I discovered in a dream in late July.

I was walking along the fifth-floor hallway where my office used to be, overlooking the Iowa River, and was delighted to see my friend Carol in her office next to mine, talking with a student. So, I ambled up and down the hall, hoping to chat with her when she finished conferring, but the last time I walked by her office she was gone and the room completely empty—no books, no bookcases, no desk, no chair. Such a disturbing experience, I immediately left the building. And then wanted to go back in to see if everything was actually as strange and unfamiliar as it seemed. I started by walking up a long outside flight of wooden steps to the fifth floor, but the steps were rickety, and the farther I climbed the more perilous it became until I was just a few steps from the top, where a raggedly dressed person I didn't recognize was reaching out to give me a hand, but I couldn't reach it and there was nothing for me to step up on. I decided to go back down, but there was a crowd of people behind me pressing to go the rest of the way up, and when I told them of the missing steps above they suddenly fled, and the steps below were suddenly gone as well, and I was left in midair gaping down in horror, at which point I awoke from the dream and immediately wrote up this account of it.

During the sixteen years of my retirement, I've never had a dream that so vividly embodies not only how distant I now feel from a world that was once the center of my existence, but also how one's aging and the ever-changing circumstances of an institution or a profession ultimately produce a disturbing gulf between one's present and one's past. I'm an outsider where I was once an insider, a stranger where I was once at home. And everything in my present experience seems to reinforce that sense of estrangement.

A few weeks before that dream, I received an email from John, who currently directs the nonfiction program, proposing to sponsor a reading of my forthcoming book at Prairie Lights. And I was touched by his solicitousness. But in the back and forth that followed, he wrote of wanting "to create for current students a sense of the heritage of the program," which made me feel somewhat like a relic, more fit for a museum than a reading. A few weeks later, I had a similar feeling when my colleague Ed asked if I'd be willing to meet with someone in the dean's office to provide historical background about the program.

In the wake of those exchanges, I found myself wishing, as I often do nowadays, that my advanced age might liberate me from thinking about my erstwhile authority or anything else of that sort. To be in the moment, completely free of self-consciousness—that would be a pleasure indeed. And it might be possible were I not keeping this log and not paying so much attention to myself. Better I should be tending my tomato plants, nothing in mind but the tang of their ripe flesh. A few days ago, the heat was so intense, as it has been the past two weeks, that I harvested several ripe tomatoes from the Golden Sunrays, lest they spoil before Jackie and I could enjoy them. So many large fruits crammed on the vines that only a delicate surgical procedure with sharp shears enabled me to remove the ripest ones without disturbing the others. The smaller Jaune Flammes hanging in panicles nearby were much easier to pick, so I filled my oak basket with orange fruit, enough to produce an ample gazpacho.

Back inside at the kitchen counter, I halved the fruit, then worked it gently back and forth across a small-toothed grater, discarding the skin, sampling the orange pulp and juice fresh from the vines, then supplementing it with red juice from my tomatoes of last summer. Then I peeled and grated three cloves of garlic from the garden and stirred the gratings into the reddish-orange juice, peeled and minced a sweet onion from the garden and stirred the mincings into the reddish-orange juice flecked with garlic, minced a pickling cucumber from the garden and stirred the mincings into the reddish-orange juice flecked with garlic and onion, de-seeded and minced a yellow pepper from the garden and stirred it into the reddish-orange juice flecked with garlic, onion, and cucumber—my eyes so bent upon the changing color of things, my taste buds so roused by the changing texture of things, that I thought of nothing but that soup. A summation of summer that I flavored with sea salt and grated pepper, stirring and tasting; paprika and pimente d'espellette, stirring and tasting; olive oil, lime juice, and tarragon white wine vinegar brewed fifteen years ago by Kate—stirring and tasting. A few more shakes of salt, stirring and tasting; a few more pinches of pimente d'espellette, stirring and tasting; a few more drops of Kate's fifteen-year-old vinegar, stirring and tasting. And then, two hours having passed with nothing on my mind but that soup and its texture and its taste, I was blessed with the thought that one might age like the tarragon in Kate's vinegar, outlasting oneself in distilled form.

I remember how she made a bouquet garni of tarragon, shoved it into a bottle she had saved from a fifth of Pescevino, funneled hot wine vinegar over the herbs, and corked the bottle tightly when it cooled down. And I remember how she prized the curvy look of that pale green, fish-shaped bottle, its tail fins, body scales and head-shaped top so distinctive, its floating herbs so alluring, that she envisioned how attractively the corked bottle of vinegar would grace the kitchen counter when she brought it up from the dark basement fruit room, where it resided for some fourteen years until I uncorked it last year. The memory of its aroma assured me I would savor the hint of her tarragon vinegar in the gazpacho that Jackie and I planned to have for dinner after it had aged several hours in the refrigerator, and the next day for lunch after it had aged overnight in the refrigerator, and the next day in memory, wishing I had made even more.

Eighty-One 🖋

Self-Sufficiency, Travel, Aging Lovebirds

AUGUST 2013 TO FEBRUARY 2014

I never imagined this chronicle might displace me while I'm still alive, but that's more or less what happened at a cancer checkup in mid September. When my oncologist entered the room, I gave him a copy of the opening piece, figuring it might be of interest, since it recalls the time when he was overseeing my chemotherapy and recovery from Hodgkin's lymphoma in 2010. But I didn't expect him to set the piece down on the examining table and start reading with such an intense focus that I felt like a bystander and the checkup like an afterthought. It was, of course, a pleasure to watch him turning the pages and to hear him respond with delight. Also, a pleasure to learn that the lymphoma is still in remission. I felt as if I could walk on air.

A few days later, on a balmy afternoon, a perfect time to be out in the garden, I was inside washing the kitchen floor. Far from walking on air, I was bent on showing Jackie I'm not as negligent a housekeeper as she thinks. Also bent on showing myself that I'm still self-sufficient enough to handle the basic tasks inside and out. But the linoleum was not getting as spotless as the TV ad for my floor-cleaning machine had led me to expect. And the vibrating gizmo was not equipped to suck up the soap that squirted on the floor through its push-button dispenser, so I would have to mop up the dirty soap-water myself. But I couldn't find the long-handled mop, leaving me no choice but to get on my hands and knees and wipe up the dirty fluid with paper towels. That's when the outraged words came to mind, "At eighty-one, I shouldn't have to be doing this kind of work." Not just once, but three times more those words resounded in my mind, each iteration more outraged than the last, my anger fed by the conviction that I was the only eighty-one-year-old in Iowa (or anywhere else for that matter), wiping up dirty water from a kitchen floor. An outlandish conviction which soon led to the bracing thought that I was in a self-indulgent spiral. I thought of my brother Marshall, whom I'd seen recently, so crippled now by the aftermath of polio sixty-five years ago that he couldn't possibly wash his kitchen floor even if he wanted to. It would probably be an exaggeration to say that the thought of my disabled brother made me grateful for the demands of my kitchen floor, but it would not be misleading to say I was intrigued by the question of whether an octogenarian should be exempt from such a task, or more broadly, whether advanced age should exempt one from onerous housecleaning tasks. Unanswerable questions of age-determined rights and responsibility made me realize I was still on a high lonesome, far from the more practical question of how to get my house clean in the absence of a cleaning service. And in this particular case, it gradually dawned on me that my floor-cleaning machine might be an excellent tool if I don't squirt too much soap fluid on the floor with its push-button dispenser.

A few days after the floor crisis, when I returned home with several bags of groceries and started to unload them from the car, a young woman sitting under the trees on my front lawn asked, "Can I carry those up to your house?" Surprised by her offer, I thanked her with the assurance that I could handle the bags myself. But I couldn't help thinking that in light of her offer, she'd probably be disturbed by the sight of me on hands and knees wiping up the kitchen floor, as would other young women and men who've gone out of their way to open doors for me at the supermarket and other public places. It must be my gray hair, for there's nothing in my posture or behavior that suggests I'm unable to manage for myself.

When it comes to such routine activities as carrying my groceries or opening doors, I've sometimes felt a bit put off by offers of assistance, even as I've been touched by such gestures of concern. This conflicted feeling helped me understand how my brother must have felt when I visited him early in September. He was so distressed by having to be pushed around in a wheelchair that he insisted on walking into a restaurant with only his cane for support, despite a difficult path from the car to the entryway. Indeed, Marshall's friend Elmer, a physically active octogenarian, is "always insulted," according to his wife Pam, "if someone offers him a seat on BART." But it's not quite as simple as wanting to be on one's own feet, or wanting to be perceived as physically capable despite one's age or infirmities, for the impulse to offer special attention to an aged or disabled person is so natural as to be irrepressible. Those different impulses sometimes lead to distressing situations, especially for someone like Marshall. Given his lifetime of self-sufficiency, even in the wake of polio, the infirmities of age must be very dispiriting.

It's also upsetting that the pricey retirement center where he and his wife Phyllis now live does not have assisted living facilities for someone with his problems, despite the center's website, which suggests that it does. Now I understand why the *Times* "New Old Age" series has a piece on the shenanigans of the retirement home industry. Jackie was only able to discover the discrepancy between the retirement center's website and its actual facilities by posing as a prospective client and questioning one of the staff. Mindful of that disturbing experience, Jackie and I vowed to enroll only in the local retirement center, Oaknoll, which definitely has complete assisted living facilities for both physical and mental disabilities. But now six months later, we've still not made any moves to do so, because we're both uneasy about the ghettoized nature of retirement communities. We prefer to continue living in our own homes, as if we could do so forever.

From what I can tell, we're not alone in our avoidance of retirement communities, given the seventy-sixth birthday party that Jackie's real-estate partner Jane threw for herself in early October, a fizzy occasion featuring not only a generous spread of food and drinks but also a performance of "Seventy-Six Trombones" by a masterful quartet of them. Yet what sticks in my mind more than anything else was the spectacle of us seventy- and eighty-year-olds, mostly in our comfortable homes, as if we might never need assisted living. As if we could high-step our way to the beat of "Seventy-Six Trombones."

A few days later, on our way into Chicago with Bill and Jan, we were talking about Jane's party, and I said it seemed as if all the guests were geezers like us, yet few of them had entered a retirement home, and Bill replied "but did you notice they were all sitting down." Strange that I hadn't noticed, but perhaps that's because I spend so much time in a chair with my laptop, whereas Bill and Jan are often on the go, on the road, traveling around Iowa for accordion get-togethers, throughout the country to visit their children (and grandchildren), and to various places in central and south America to sample the food, the culture, and the architecture, which Bill records in vivid pen-and-inks. How different from Jackie and me, for we rarely do more than three or four trips a year, so while this weekend in Chicago is a special occasion for us, Bill and Jan will be off to the southwest just four days after getting home from Chicago.

Perhaps we'd travel more if Jackie weren't working full time, but I couldn't imagine traveling as much as Bill and Jan do, while still tending my gardens and this chronicle. Nor could I deal with an arrangement like that of Mike and Judy, whom we visited in Chicago, where Mike has an apartment and spends most of the workweek managing his investment business, though they live in Saugatuck, Michigan, where Judy is a designer. So, they're only together on the weekends. But that's the way it is with Jackie and me, except when she comes over for dinner once or twice during the workweek. What it comes down to, I guess, is that most of us in our seventies and eighties have distinctive living and travel arrangements, though few as unusual as Don and Dorothy's, he retired from the psych department here, she from Iowa State, and both so devoted to retaining their 100,000 air-mile status that they're often in the skies just for a weekend.

Speaking of travel, in early November Jackie and I had a magical twelve days in Costa Rica, lured there by images of exotic fauna and flora, by red-eyed tree frogs and blue morpho butterflies, pink bamboo orchids and lavender forest lilies. A tropical wonderland, Costa Rica's lush rain forests and black sand beaches dazzled us and our tour group. I can still see a large tarantula spider scampering away from a tarantula hawk wasp, thanks to Jackie's beady eyes. Still see an egret on a riverbank, oblivious of a crocodile coming up behind it. And still feel the exhilaration of being closer to paradise than ever before, when I was walking above the trees in a rainforest, gazing down at their orchid-covered branches, unruffled by the swaying bridge under my feet or a lifetime fear of heights. Free at last from acrophobia! Or so it seemed until the prospect of doing the zip line left me standing on the forest floor while Jackie ventured that midair walk before any of the others in our group. That's when they discovered what I have come to know—that her gracious and engaging manner goes hand in hand with a fearless spirit. No wonder they toasted her at our farewell dinner.

In Costa Rica, as in our tour of northern Italy, I was the only octogenarian in a group of sixty- and seventy-year-olds and for the most part felt as capable and vigorous as the others, except when it came to walking the long, steep upland paths of the rain forest, my heart and lungs straining to deal with the incline. A painful reminder of the clear-cut limits in my life, which made me sympathize with a host tree suffocating in the midst of a strangler fig. The rain forest, after all, is fraught with images of life under stress, of the understory struggling for light, just as I was struggling for air. But my uphill problem was trivial compared to the impediments of others on the tour, especially Harry, a seventy-six-year-old retired physics professor with a severely damaged leg from a fall in the Grand Canyon, who soldiered his way up and down the paths with two canes. I was also touched by Harry's reflections on his experience: "Whenever anyone goes through difficult passages in marriage or life, they either adapt and thrive or they break apart." Though he credited that wisdom to Gail Sheehy, I could see he had lived it himself, as have countless others whose mantra is "adapt and thrive."

It's one thing to hear such wisdom but quite another to behold it in strangers, especially in a place like Costa Rica, where one's attention is often focused instead on tropical flowers and exotic creatures. I'm thinking especially of Isaac, a sixty-five-year-old former laborer who had transformed his life and the life of his family by training himself to become an orchid gardener. He then developed his own orchid garden and rain forest preserve, where I admired his diminutive orchids, butterfly garden, and the sighting of that panicked tarantula. But I was impressed most of all by Isaac himself, his extensive knowledge of rain-forest plants, his self-effacing manner, and his striking family—wife, son, granddaughter, and father—all thriving, thanks to him, in that Edenic setting. On leaving the garden, I shook the hand of Isaac's diminutive, 101-year-old father, whose eyes lit up at the moment of our encounter, as did mine.

There were other memorable people along the way, but none quite so impressive as our native guide Max. Born to a farming family, he might have spent his life working the land near the small village where he was raised. But Max was captivated by the sight of a rain forest when he was eight years old, then longed for a life in the forest, longed to be where he could continue to see the exotic birds and other creatures. So, as a young man he moved to the city of San José to attend the University of Costa Rica, where he studied biology and microbiology and, later, eco-tourism, gradually becoming a knowledgeable guide and specialist in the development of national parks. He is also one of the most articulate speakers of English I've ever heard, regaling us on our long bus rides from place to place with a history of Costa Rica and with stories of his life. An epitome of how profoundly one's destiny can be shaped by a memorable childhood experience, a consuming ambition, and an opportune education.

In an earlier version of this piece, after writing about Costa Rica, I spent four paragraphs detailing my current maladies, especially the sudden onset of severe arthritis, but when Jackie read that segment she told me to "cut the weepies, otherwise people will shut the book and stop reading." Jackie, as must be clear by now, prefers to look on the brighter side than I, and in this case I deferred to her opinion, given how my cancer nurse Patti greeted me during her recent checkup: "You don't look like you're eighty; you don't look eighty at all!" To which I wanted to reply, "But I sure feel like it!" Yet I didn't actually have any idea of how people typically feel at eighty, so I said nothing and blushed like a flattered schoolboy.

On the other hand, Jackie's opinion of things is not unerring, as I noticed during a recent disagreement. We were out shopping when she announced, "You need to stock up on toilet paper. You've been running low for a long time." Which struck me as an exaggeration, so I asked: "Isn't a twelve-pack enough?" And to my surprise, she said, "When I get down to twelve, that's a sign that I'm running low, and it's time to buy more." Which led me to ask, "Are you stockpiling against a paper shortage?" No sooner did I ask that question than I realized we were having an argument that could only take place between two aging lovebirds, set in their ways and duking it out over toilet paper.

I never imagined such an argument when we got together ten years ago. I remember instead our first date, a few days after the new year began, first to see *Calendar Girls*, then to have dinner at my place, where we supped on broiled chicken breasts basted with a mixture of low-salt tamari sauce, lime juice, grated garlic, and olive oil, so juicy and tangy that I paired it with a platter of thin spaghetti, dressed very simply in olive oil, salt, minced parsley, and grated parmesan, balanced by an equally simple salad of romaine and sweet onions in a vivid white wine vinaigrette. And then we talked for hours without a single disagreement. I also remember a moment later that year, our honeymoon year, when Jackie, fretting about my maladies, made a surprising request, "Just give me ten good years." A request that led me to write her a ten-line poem in ten-syllable lines for our tenth anniversary, January 4, 2014.

TEN YEARS

"Ten years," you said, "Just give me ten good years,"
As if I or anyone could assure you
Such a thing without divine assistance.
As if terms could be set and years prescribed
Without forsaking far far more than years.
For now that ten have come and gone, what next
Would you ask for? Another ten good ones?
As if we two should parcel out our lives
In decades? Dear Jackie, the love we have,
The special life we share, transcends such bounds.

I wonder what I'll write her ten years from now, assuming we're both here and still arguing about toilet paper or other such things.

A month later during a visit to our friends Dick and Phyllis, who winter in Rancho Mirage, I noticed how they get along like lovebirds without the hint of an argument about anything, sharing all the household chores of cooking, shopping, housecleaning, and caring for their dog. But I also noticed how busily Dick preoccupies himself every day in so many different ways that he's like a perpetual motion machine, rarely sitting down to relax except to read the newspaper. Which moved me to ask him about his busyness, and he told me with considerable intensity in his voice that "you've got to keep busy, you've got to keep doing things, otherwise you're in trouble." "What kind of trouble?" I wanted to ask, but didn't pursue the matter, because I could see that I'd touched a nerve.

Given Dick's prior work as chief executive of a large and successful food-marketing business, I wonder if retirement has left him empty-handed, particularly when he's away from Iowa City, where he engages in a wide range of generous volunteer activities. Or to consider his situation in a larger context, I wonder if a lifetime of work leaves us unfit for the satisfactions of a leisurely existence. Or is it simply a matter of temperament rather than the influence of a working life? Though Jackie is still working full time, she's driven to polish every shining minute, even when she comes to my place for the weekend. So, I suppose she'll keep busy even in retirement, assuming of course that she ever retires. Whereas I'm so distractible that even in the course of working on this chronicle I'm tempted to visit the internet for stock market updates, email messages, and *New York Times* headlines.

But sometimes all it takes to get me writing is a memorable get-together, like a Valentine's dinner party that Phyllis prepared for eight of us, all in our mid seventies to mid eighties, all of us brightened by a few drinks, her elegant table of hearts and flowers, a tasty leg of lamb, and a lively conversation. The only problem is that the conversation veered, as it often does among folks our age, toward the misfortune of others our age whose lives have taken a turn for the worse. Like a variation on *schadenfreude*. Though each gloomy tale was resonant with a concern for the well-being of friends or relatives, I couldn't help wondering whether such tales might also be animated by an unconscious pleasure in out-thriving or out-living others of our generation. Longevity, after all, is a universally celebrated goal, implicit not only in the sadness of those tales, but also in the life-saving efforts of advanced medical care. But it was Valentine's Day, so I kept those thoughts to myself.

A week later in Iowa City during a dinner party at Carrie's, the conversation again veered toward the ill-fated lives of others our age but without any of the usual pieties. In fact, Rebecca compared our situation to "a slow boat on the river Styx." But that brief bit of black humor gave way to somber expressions when we learned about the imminent demise of our friend Bob, who has often seemed in such good health that his sudden reversal of fortune—an incurable brain tumor—was too close for everyone's comfort. And the conversation soon moved on to savory matters like Carrie's tangy dessert cake with rhubarb sauce and ice cream.

Maybe it's just the weather that has me fixated on such chill topics, for it turns out to have been Iowa's coldest winter in thirty-five years, and one of the coldest in 120 years of record keeping. And we haven't yet seen what March will bring. Whatever it brings, this much is clear: the big chill is inevitable and so are litanies of its chilling effects. And that's a truth that even Jackie cannot deny.

Eighty-One to Eighty-Two ✍
Illusions, Compulsions, Studious Smiles

MARCH 2014 TO AUGUST 2014

My brother Marshall called in mid August with the best news of the past several months, for there he was on the other end of the line, sounding better than he has in years, thanks to a drug called Aricept. Fluent and precise, he told me, "I'm now taking part in a discussion group that meets once a week, and I can speak so well that I say more than anyone in the group. And people now come to my table to dine and talk with me during lunch and dinner." A striking transformation, for when we spoke last month his conversation was fragmented and his usage sometimes off base, so I had to decipher what he said in order to make sense of it. Now he's as articulate as when he was a preeminent neonatal researcher and worldwide lecturer on mother/infant bonding. I'm awed by the power of a ten-milligram pill to improve a condition that's afflicted him for several years, though I realize, as the drug manufacturer makes clear, that Aricept improves the symptoms but does not slow the progression of Alzheimer's disease. Though I'm delighted by the change, I'm troubled by the reversal that's sure to come. Yet I'm also grateful for whatever he gains from the pill, no matter how brief the benefits.

When I started making notes for this piece in early March, my arthritic knees and gouty toe were so painful I hobbled around the house. A few months earlier I'd been sauntering above the treetops in a Costa Rican rain forest and hiking the trails below as if nothing could impede me except an occasional shortness of breath. How could I have turned into a cripple so quickly, without anything to explain it or forebode it? A puzzling question, until I realized the pain that beset me on the treadmill back in February was the climax of an aging process that had been going on slowly for many years, so I didn't anticipate it. How age deceives us and we deceive ourselves with illusions of aging without aging! The cartilage in my knees had been wearing away every day, as it does with everyone in the course of aging. But the last time I had knee problems, some twenty years ago, the orthopedist's suggestion to lose weight, exercise, and take over-the-counter pain relievers had worked so well that the pain not only disappeared but also remained in abeyance even after I stopped taking them. Lulled by such a comforting lack of symptoms, I assumed my condition had been remedied, when in fact it was much worse, as my orthopedist showed me via x-ray, describing it bluntly as "bone on bone." That vivid image led me to think my gardening days might soon be over, and that I might be destined for an assisted living center. Yet in mid August, just five months later, I'm again back on my feet, exercising on the treadmill, digging and weeding in the garden, walking up and down the stairs several times a day. Oh yes, I needed a few months to recover, and even now I'm slow to bend down, slower still to rise from a kneeling position, and can only keep the knee pain at bay with daily doses of arthritis-strength Tylenol. Minor adjustments given my continued mobility, and soothing evidence of the body's resilience. Indeed, I'm almost tempted to believe my knees will not trouble me again, especially since I've heeded my orthopedist's command not to incline the treadmill, for that's what stressed them out in February. Yet how convenient to blame the incline rather than face up to the certainties of aging, and then having relinquished the incline how convenient to ignore the loss of its cardiovascular benefits.

My mind plays such tricks on me it sometimes seems as if I've become a master of rationalization, but even Jackie has illusions about the condition of her aging body. How else to account for her surprise that a bone density test revealed she has osteopenia (low bone density) but not osteoporosis. "Good news," according to her internist, but disarming to Jackie, who evidently supposed she could age without her bones aging at all. What we can't see or don't feel we don't heed, as if our skin might wrinkle and our hair turn gray without anything akin taking place inside. Talking of illusions, a few months ago I was watching a TV program on aging that featured a University of Iowa professor of leisure studies who declared that "avoidance of disease and disability is fundamental to successful aging," as if disease and disability were not inevitable aspects of advanced age, successful or otherwise. I wonder what the professor would think about Roger Angell's bracing account of his infirmities and maladies in "This Old Man" (*The New Yorker*, Feb. 17, 2014). Many of mine are the same as Angell's, which made me think we have at least one thing in common, though I'm eighty-two and he's ninety-four—both of us exemplifying the unavoidable aspects of aging the professor considers avoidable. Which also makes me wonder how he might rationalize his notion of "successful aging" for my colleague Bob, who succumbed to the brain tumor in mid April that had just been discovered in January, but not before giving a reading and discussion from his last book in late March.

Given the swiftness and achievement of Bob's final months, the time that's left seems all the more precious. So, I'm concerned with what to make of it, especially after reading a *New York Times* obituary that felt like a rebuke of my recent days and ways. It told about the life of Anthony Smith, a British author and adventurer, who at the age of eighty-three crossed the Atlantic with three other old men on a handmade raft, archly named "Antiki." When asked about his reason for launching such an audacious venture several years ago, he echoed a line from T. S. Eliot's "East Coker" in *Four Quartets*—"Old men ought to be explorers"—and then declared

"Am I supposed to potter about, pruning roses . . . or should I do something to justify my existence?" His scorn of tending a garden brought me up short when I read it just a day after taking stock of my backyard and logging a self-congratulatory note about it for this piece: "First time all spring and summer the yard has been completely under control. My weeding and fussing have been so effective, I'd be happy to spend the rest of the summer keeping it trimmed." Betrayed by my own words, I felt like a slacker compared to Smith, who rafted across the Atlantic and back despite being crippled and dependent on two canes. And it didn't get any better when Jackie brought me a piece by Oliver Sacks, "The Joy of Turning 80," in *AARP The Magazine*, where he declares "I am sorry I have wasted (and still waste) so much time." If Sacks thinks himself wasteful, I must be profligate.

On the other hand, why should I apologize for cultivating my garden when it brings forth an abundance of broccoli, lettuce, onions, eggplants, peppers, and tomatoes? Nothing wasteful about that. And the same goes for keeping this chronicle, since its record of experience and reflection might bear fruit for others with an interest in the nature of life during one's ninth decade. But rather than belabor these defensive remarks, I'm interested in what my sensitivity on this score might suggest about the psychological pressures one feels during this period of life, especially when reading the obits, pondering what one's life might look like in a final write-up. I sense in myself and in many of my aged friends a fierce impulse to be productive, to be useful, or as Smith put it "to justify my existence"—an echo of which I've heard in Jackie's impatience with "people our age who sit around doing nothing." As if devoting one's latter days to smelling the roses were an abuse of one's existence. Indeed, Jackie continues to work full time and says, "It has nothing to do with the money; if I weren't working, I sometimes feel I'd cease to exist." An existential imperative! Maybe that's what Dick meant that day in Rancho Mirage, when he told me, "You've got to keep busy; you've got to keep doing things, otherwise you're in trouble." But it might also be a compulsion engendered by a lifetime of work, which ill prepares us for a life of leisure.

I was struck by that compulsion in myself when Jackie urged me to deal with several large boxes of stuff I had brought home from my study in the university library, gathering dust in the TV room the past two years. I promised to sort through it all and file things either in my attic study or the trash. Probably the latter, given her sensible advice about an octogenarian's need to get rid of the clutter before taking leave of this world. But every time I opened one of the boxes and started going through the manila folders, everything I found there (manuscripts, syllabi, publishers' correspondence, typescripts of professional talks) was so bound up with my career that I didn't want to throw any of it away. But I also couldn't ignore the likelihood that neither I nor anyone else would be interested in any of those folders in years to come, since I had completely ignored them in years gone by. How strange to think that what had once seemed important no longer compelled my attention or interest.

Those thoughts came to mind again a month later, when my granddaughter Kathleen and her husband Jeff came to visit for a few days, both of them working on their doctoral dissertations and both so concerned about getting jobs, getting published, and getting established in their profession that those subjects dominated much of their conversation. But their intense professional concerns reminded me of my own some fifty-five years ago, and thus we were united across the generations, which made me think they too might someday look back upon this time in their lives with comparable bemusement.

What I never imagined when I was their age is that I would live long enough to enjoy the company of adult grandchildren—a special gift of advanced age that I've come to realize from Kathleen and Jeff's visits the past few years, as well as the visits of my other granddaughter, Lizzie. Though they put me in mind of my youthful days, they also remind me of how differently we've come of age, especially given the digital wonders of their generation, as Kathleen made clear one afternoon when I was looking in the phone book for the number of an out-of-town restaurant. "You're using a phone book to track down a number? How utterly nineties!" Not until that moment did I realize how far behind the times I am, given my lack of a smartphone, an iPad, or any other of the digital gadgets that have shifted people's attention from immediate experience to screens. But then again, when my grandson Ben came to visit earlier this month, on his way to become a golf pro in San Francisco, we had a lively conversation about reading and writing and other shared interests that made me feel more capable of bridging the age gap.

Whomever I'm with, whatever their age, my mind, it seems, is more in the moment these days, or in spots of time, recent or past, that are still vivid, like a lunch with Jackie in mid May. We were eating on the terrace, munching on a salad I had made of crisp romaine hearts, chopped sweet onions, cucumbers, orange peppers, albacore tuna, and yellow tomatoes, dressed with an olive oil, lemon, and Dijon mustard vinaigrette—tangy, crunchy, and colorful, accompanied with pita chips, that Jackie oohed and aahed over. But a few minutes later, she posed a question that took me by surprise: "Given how happy we often claim to be, I wonder why we aren't any happier than we seem to be." I was surprised in part because her deftly worded question was out of context, like a sudden cloudburst on a sunny day. Surprised as well because it's not what I would expect from someone who's often in such a good mood that her default expression is a smile. Then again, I couldn't help noting how tired she'd been that week, and I too, both of us beset by wakeful nights and the unpleasantly cool days of this chilly spring.

When I mentioned those wakeful nights, Jackie dismissed them out of hand, pointing the finger at me and my frequently hangdog expression: "You always look so gloomy even when there's cause for joy that it makes me think you're perpetually out of sorts." Though I might have contested the "always," there's no doubting the gloomy cast of my face, especially in youthful snapshots, my head down as if embarrassed. Yet I also felt compelled to mention how the sadness of my childhood had evidently left its mark in an aversion to the camera, for how else to explain the downward tilt of my head in all those early shots. On the other hand, I also noted that in the years since then my brother has often seemed so bright eyed and sunny that he must have willed himself to be so, to serve the needs of his work with mothers and newborn children. Which made me wonder why I hadn't cultivated a genial smile to suit my classroom teaching, like my long-ago department chair whose perpetual smile made me and other colleagues wonder if he smiled when completely alone. Had my youthful sadness cast my face in gloom? Have I frowned so long my gloom is cast in stone?

That lunchtime episode led me to imagine a brief exercise that might help me smile more often, or at least overcome the gloomy cast of my face. Immediately after shaving, I imagined myself standing for ten minutes in front of the bathroom mirror, smiling. First a warm-up smile, involving just the mouth, otherwise known as a false smile or Pan Am smile, from the stewardesses of yore who flashed it on and off with ease. Then a full smile, involving both the mouth and eyes, so wide as to produce a bright-eyed, crinkly expression, known as the Duchenne smile, after the nineteenth-century French neurologist who first identified it. Practicing those two smiles for ten minutes every morning, I imaged myself becoming so adept at smiling it would gradually become habitual. A fanciful regimen to be sure, and too late to make a difference. Given current neurological and psychological research suggesting a connection not only between smiling and happiness but also between smiling and longevity, I wish it was possible for me to smile like my former department chairman, who lived to be ninety-five.

Speaking of looks and longevity, ever since Jackie and I got together some ten years ago, she has urged me to get my Jeep detailed—"Aren't you embarrassed to be driving something so messy and dirty?" She might also have asked if I'm not embarrassed to be driving something so aged and rusty, given that it's now eighteen years old, a centenarian in car-years. I understand, of course, why she keeps her car so clean and up to date, given the need to drive her real-estate clients around town in proper fashion. And pangs of guilt do beset me whenever I remember the first sight of my custom-built Jeep Grand Cherokee, its moss green body aglow, its tan leather seats, and black dashboard spotless. But having an immaculate vehicle has never seemed to me important enough to spend the money on detailing, so I've done nothing more than run it through a car wash once or twice a year and occasionally vacuum the front and back seats or take a wet rag to the dashboard. No surprise, then, that my Jeep has been looking as shabby as Jackie says. Still, I was taken aback recently when she said, "It's looking so bad I'll pay to have it detailed for your birthday."

Not the birthday present of my dreams. Yet how could I refuse, though I couldn't help thinking it might look somewhat ridiculous to have a spotlessly clean car with rusted-out rocker panels below all the doors. The thought of that disconnect led me on a merry-go-round of local body shops, in hope of getting the rust removed and new panels installed. But a recurring estimate of "about four thousand" led me to decide I could live with the rusted-out panels, much as I live with my rusting knee joints, especially after one of the shop owners told me "you'd be a fool to waste all that money when the rust'll come back as sure as the rain and the snow." Having settled that matter, I spent a few hours decluttering the Jeep, replacing the old floor pads with new ones and touching up some of the scratch marks with new paint before driving it to Steve the detailer. I told him, "It's not a precious antique, so don't fuss over it." When he said that "touching up the paint and buffing some of the spots might improve things a bit," I didn't expect anything special. Just a very clean car, with some of its scratches concealed but its rust unchanged.

But when Steve opened the gate at the back of his driveway, it seemed as if he had magically rolled back eighteen years, for there was my Jeep, its moss green body aglow like it was the day I first saw it. Which distracted my attention from the rust, making me smile without even thinking about it. A full Duchenne smile! And the interior was equally striking, as if it had never been dusty or dirty or grimy, a transformation that led Steve to explain: "That moss green color really surprised me with the depth of its glow." And it was the same with Jackie, who declared the change "miraculous." Which made me wish that I too could be detailed and miraculously transformed—to look and feel as I did some eighteen years ago when I first beheld the Jeep. No longer a retired geezer but a still active professor. Yet no sooner did I imagine such a change than I realized it would also involve the resurrection of Kate, who had been standing by my side when I first beheld the Jeep. The thought of that implausibility dispelled my fantasy as quickly as it had emerged, and refocused my attention on the rusted rocker panels. Still, I couldn't stop smiling at the glow of the Jeep, and at the irrepressible desire to reclaim some measure of one's glowing past, a hope that burns in all of us from time to time.

A few weeks later, the future that haunts us led Jackie and me to dinner with our friend Jean at Oaknoll, the retirement home we've been thinking about with all the mixed feelings of an approach-avoidance conflict. From the moment we entered the dining room and saw the featured entrée of baked sea bass and then the full menu, we were pleasantly surprised by the wide range of other appealing entrées, salads, and sandwiches, as in a first-class restaurant. We ordered the bass, and it turned out to be as good as it looked, served on a bed of sautéed scallions and yellow tomatoes. And when Jean asked one of the waiters for rolls, he swiftly arrived with two different kinds, both warm.

An after-dinner tour of Jean's apartment surprised us again, for we found it more spacious and gracious than any accommodations we'd seen there in years past, thanks to Oaknoll's recent building and remodeling program. I began to wish that I too were ensconced in such a light, bright, and airy space, with an inviting study, a comfortable bedroom, a trim kitchen, a large living room, and an enclosed balcony overlooking an inner courtyard. Jackie felt the same way, so she stopped at the information desk on the way out to pick up a packet of stuff about the place. A few days later, though, I couldn't imagine myself at Oaknoll and neither could Jackie. Even after a summer on my arthritic knees, struggling with the weeds in my vegetable gardens and perennial beds, I'm still not ready to call it quits, still not ready to abandon the backyard. And as it turns out, Oaknoll doesn't project any vacancies until 2022, by which time I might already be gone.

Though neither of us is ready for the cozy but age-bound world of Oaknoll, we've both decided that we're no longer up to the challenges of overseas travel. A tour of Turkey we had booked made us uneasy, after a friend canceled one herself because of State Department advisories. Beyond the scary political turbulence in and around Turkey, both of us admitted we've lost our tolerance for the hassles and stresses of long-distance air travel, such as an eleven-hour nonstop flight from Chicago to Istanbul. Even after our seven-hour flight last year from Chicago to Costa Rica, I understood why I was the only eighty-year-old on that tour. Age, after all, has narrowed our horizons, and there are places I once longed to visit that I'll never see. But I've never had a bucket list, and as Jackie said in consolation, "There are many places in this country we've never seen." So, we've trimmed our sails and are heading up to a little cabin on Lake Superior at the end of this month. A remote and pristine spot where we've hiked before and supped on the pleasures of a simpler life than in any other place I've known.

A week up north, I hope, will also help me forget a visit to the memory unit of a local retirement home, where a former graduate student and collaborator is now living. She was once so articulate and vivacious, such an accomplished writer and teacher, it's difficult to believe that a rare brain condition has reduced her to uttering brief repetitions or slight variations of whatever one says to her. Like a robot. Or, as often, she says nothing at all. But she's clearly there somewhere, given how warmly she extended her hand to take hold of mine, and how she opened her arms to be hugged when Jackie and I were on the verge of leaving. We've watched her decline the past two years since she returned to Iowa City from her last academic position, but no amount of familiarity with her condition makes me any more accustomed to it. In fact, our visit to her in this setting, where she's recently been moved, made me even more dismayed, given how far out of reach she is compared to others we met there. Some of them are so genial and talkative, I asked Jackie why they were living in such a place, and she set me straight: "It's a continuum, and if you spend any time with them, you'll see they belong there."

Yet what a place to belong in! The very thought of it left me wondering where Jackie and I might belong in the years to come, a haunting question that made me eager for the distractions of Lake Superior.

Before we drove north, my thoughts turned elsewhere, thanks to our friend Joe, a masterful artist who invited us to see his studio and sit for a series of drawings he's been working on. When he's not drawing, Joe works in oil, producing meticulously detailed images based on photographs of the street markets in Oaxaca—images in which he seeks to evoke the qualities of that distinctive place. His work involves such different media, subjects, and styles, I admire his unusual artistic versatility and his ability to carry on a lively conversation, sometimes a spirited monologue, in the process of drawing, whereas I can hardly walk and talk at the same time. Though he's just a few years younger than Jackie and I, he's more vigorous and resourceful by far. And more versatile too, as he moves from a drawing of Jackie to one of me, then Jackie again, then me again, combining pencil, pastel, and ink as the spirit moves him, erasing and redrawing as his intuition guides him—visual improvisation! Each drawing quite different from the other, as if he's seen each of us anew, each of us in a distinctly different light, or seen a different side of us in each case. Hearing him talk while he works, telling us about his devotion to choral singing, I wonder if he might burst forth in song. A manifold artist, undaunted by age.

Eighty-Two 🖎
Money, Infirmities, Injury, Forgetfulness

AUGUST 2014 TO FEBRUARY 2015

I've been comfortably retired for so many years, thanks to an annuity, an IRA, and Social Security, that I never imagined anyone would want to read about such routine financial matters. But Jackie told me "nothing's routine when it comes to money." My editor and friend Holly was even more pointed: "You haven't said anything about money, a subject that would surely be of interest to your readers." Here, then, is a brief summary. I'm living on about $75,000 a year after taxes: fifty-five percent from an annuity, thirty percent from Social Security, five percent from my IRA, and ten percent from book royalties. There used to be several thousand more when all my books were in print, but I still have more than enough for a single person, living alone in a house I once owned before giving it to the National Trust for Historic Preservation.

Simple and comfortable as it sounds, I spend an undue amount of time fussing over my IRA, which I've managed myself the past thirteen years. Before then, it was in a stock account managed by the College Retirement Equities Fund, but the market collapse of 2002 led to such a precipitous decline that I decided to handle things myself. A loony decision that could only have been made by someone ignorant of the stock market. In the years since then, I've learned enough to almost double the value of my IRA, while also withdrawing about five percent from it every month, but not without making so many foolish decisions along the way that I attribute most of my success to good luck and fortuitous timing rather than good judgment.

All of which is to say that I wouldn't advise anyone other than a financial savant to think of managing their own IRA. Advanced age has made me so fretful that I regularly check on the performance of individual stocks, researching alternative holdings, weighing the pros and cons of high dividend stocks vs. exchange-traded funds vs. a licensed investment counselor. Though Jackie's proud of my success and tells me that researching the market keeps me "mentally alert and widely informed," it's a time-consuming activity that could be abandoned by replacing all my holdings with something like Vanguard's broad market exchange-traded fund (VTI)—a low-cost, low-risk fund with an excellent track record. But I'm uneasy about buying into a broad market index when the market's overpriced as it is these days. And even if I did simplify things with VTI, I'd probably continue to obsess over its performance.

Currently, I have enough income to afford an idyllic getaway every year in a rented cabin on Lake Superior, where Jackie and I spend a week or two in early September. The place we had last fall was so close to the water that we dined in sight of waves lapping the shore—a perfect setting for the fresh-lake trout fillets I bought at the Dockside Fish Market in Grand Marais, Minnesota, and baked after slathering them with a briefly precooked mixture of olive oil, crushed garlic, Dijon mustard, minced scallions, and minced parsley, topped with lemon slices. A pleasure to behold and to savor after twelve minutes in the oven, and as easy to prepare as the couscous I served with them, together with a fresh spinach salad. Everything as straightforward as the lake, including the wild raspberries we picked for dessert from the bushes bordering the cabin.

Coming and going we savored the berries. And savored the nearby trails, though they're more challenging than in years past, even for Jackie. The ups and downs of the pathway keep me focused, in the moment itself, my mind issuing silent commands—"Step sideways, then down. Look at that branch, a good walking stick. Dodge that puddle and the mud beside it." Making and heeding those commands is both a healthy mental discipline and a way of quickly involving myself in the north woods. Others walk past us as if they need no such commands. And neither do I when chatting with Jackie about flowers or critters or mushrooms along the trail. The sight of such things, or the possibility of seeing them, keeps me focused on the trail. A pleasurable discipline for a distractible octogenarian.

But pleasurable distractions soon arise, like where to dine for lunch. The Angry Trout? The Crooked Spoon? The Gunflint Tavern? Restaurants as captivating as their names. And other nearby lures, like "World's Best Donuts," are just a few steps away from the bay in Grand Marais. I've been visiting that little town for twenty-five years, first with Kate, now with Jackie, and one of its most distinctive appeals, aside from its pristine bay and fresh fish store, is its unchanging facade. The same shops and restaurants from one year to the next, as if untouched by time and change, embody an endless summer dream, even when the vacation comes right after Labor Day, when the leaves up north start turning so early they belie the summer's dream.

Back home in mid September, I was struck by the sight of my drought-ridden pepper and tomato plants, emblems of how lazy a gardener I've become, neither watering nor mulching my crops to protect them from the summer heat and dryness, as I had done in seasons past. Critter-damaged broccoli plants revealed that my protective fencing had evidently been breached, but I hadn't bothered to look for the spots and block the holes, or to plant seeds for a fall crop of lettuce and other greens. The vegetable garden hadn't looked that neglected before our time up north, but there's nothing like going away to get a new perspective on things. In this case it enabled me to see what I hadn't faced up to before—that I'm no longer an attentive vegetable gardener, that my commitment to growing and tending things has waned the past few years. I haven't even ordered seeds for this spring. All of which makes me wonder how much longer I can continue to live on this three-quarter-acre lot that requires persistent care I no longer have the energy or will to provide.

While my energy has been waning, the deer have been waxing—a herd of twelve, feeding on everything that's not fenced, from the daylily and hosta beds to the yews and other edible bushes. Such a large herd is emblematic of how much the immediate environment has changed during the forty-five years since Kate and I moved onto this lot and longed to behold a deer in our backyard. Ten years we waited for our first brief sighting in the midst of a severe winter that brought a lone buck looking to graze. It bounded off at the sight of us. Now the herd is so tame, they barely move when I shoo them away, staring at me as if I were out of place rather than they. And perhaps I am. Talk about change! Those deer remind me not only of how much has changed in my backyard but also of how much has changed in the circumstances of my life, revealing how much my control of things—or illusion of control—has dwindled in recent years.

In one way or another, advanced age presages the ultimate loss of control that's implicit in mortality. Whether it's my slow recall, diminished hearing, erectile dysfunction, or osteoarthritis, I feel the losses as distinctly as I can see those deer. But something deep within me resists the poet's urge to rage about them, especially after reading Oliver Sacks's calm acceptance of his terminal cancer in a *New York Times* article. My problems, after all, are trivial compared to his and to the existential predicament confronted by our friend Burns when he was diagnosed with esophageal cancer—give up eating or give up talking. Burns chose to keep talking, but I've never heard him utter a complaint about his liquid diet. Burns's decision humbled me, for had I been faced with a similar ultimatum, I'd have succumbed to my appetite. Burns, on the other hand, not only restrains himself but indulges those of us who indulge our taste buds. For a Halloween get-together at his downtown condo, Burns arranged to have food available for us from the take-out restaurant below his place. We didn't go trick-or-treating, but we did look down from his lofty place and behold the costumed undergraduates roaming the streets below, a quirky reminder of my grizzled perspective.

We were joined by Dick and Joyce, also aged residents of the Towers on the same floor as Burns, so it was not surprising that after-dinner conversation turned to the question of how we might deal with the infirmities of advanced age, looming in the not-so-distant future for all of us. Burns, Dick, and Joyce spoke of hiring a full-time, live-in companion, rather than having to endure the retirement-home spectacle of aged debility. That image, or something very much like it, was on Jackie's mind a few days before Halloween, when she looked at me solemnly after dinner one evening and voiced a decision I couldn't reject: "I think we better sign up for Oaknoll and put down a deposit while we're still healthy enough to qualify." But on the way home from Burns's place, I wondered what Jackie thought of a live-in companion instead of Oaknoll's assisted living option, and her response was irrefutable: "That sort of arrangement is never as simple as you think, even if you have enough money to afford it. Besides, if you need assisted living, you need a lot more than any single person can provide." No masquerading for Jackie. Halloween was over.

Halloween, in fact, had been overcast and I downcast through much of October, following the death of my colleague Jix, with whom I had collaborated on numerous academic projects that influenced my choice of a career in nonfiction writing. Having seen him a couple of months before his demise, at a cocktail party where he was wry and wise as always, it was dismaying to see him prone on a couch two days before he died of leukemia, cared for by hospice, attended by family, and breathing with the help of an oxygen line. But the minute I entered his room, he sat up and held forth so genially—about writing and teaching and colleagues of yore, as well as his Welsh heritage, centuries back—that he seemed capable of lasting for weeks or months or more. Thanks to his lively and engaging performance, I had not imagined the imminence of his demise, though it was there for anyone to see. A hail and farewell I'll never forget. Now, thanks to Jix, I realize that a special benefit of advanced age is to be schooled by our dearest friends and relatives in the art of taking one's leave.

I've also been schooled in some cautionary methods of sticking around, thanks to my doctors, who have warned me off all the nostrums I once blithely took without an awareness of their risks. No more ibuprofen, naproxen, or other nonsteroidal anti-inflammatory drugs for knee pain, back pain, and other discomforts. Too risky for people like me with high blood pressure, heart disease, and kidney disease. Now I'm restricted to Tylenol and only in moderation, but it does the job without any side effects. Most sleep aids are also risky for me—and ineffective. But melatonin, a hormone produced by the pineal gland, has solved all my sleeping problems. On the recommendation of my clinical pharmacologist, I now take it nightly in a three-milligram pill, thirty minutes before bedtime—a small dose, but enough to help me sleep through the night with only one or two wake-ups for a trip to the bathroom. And it has no side effects, which makes me wonder why melatonin is not more widely advised or prescribed, since research suggests it's not only an effective sleep aid but also an effective antioxidant, more so than vitamin E.

I wish there were also a hormone to overcome forgetfulness and all the other ills our minds are heir to. A mental panacea! I imagined such a wondrous thing when my friend Stan was telling me how he'd been saved from the aftereffects of a stroke by the clot-busting drug tPA—tissue plasminogen activator—a drug that can reduce or alleviate some of the worst impairments if it's administered within three to four hours of a clot-induced stroke, the sooner the better. Stan was saved by the alertness of his wife, Pat, who called 911 shortly after onset of his stroke. At the hospital he was injected with tPA after tests that revealed a clot and its location. Two months later, Stan told me about the remarkable effects of tPA, which enabled him to sense the consecutive return of his various cognitive abilities, as if a set of switches had gradually been turned on in his brain. Stan's swift recovery had a disturbing counterpoint in the story of our friend Peter, a gifted artist and photographer, who tripped, fell on his head, and suffered a concussion, followed by surgery to relieve pressure on his brain that left him so debilitated it was months before he was eligible for rehabilitative care, and months more before his admirable willpower enabled him to recover enough to tell us about his journey back from that harrowing fall.

Closer to home, on a far less traumatic level, I've been witnessing such willpower in Jackie, who called a few weeks ago one early afternoon, her voice a bit fuzzy as she told me, "I had an accident." Her announcement made me think she was talking about her car, but after a long pause, she went on to say, "This morning I slipped and fell on a patch of ice and hurt my wrist. Can you come to my place at 4:30 this afternoon and drive me to the emergency room for an x-ray?" Given Jackie's kneejerk resistance to timely medical care, I surmised that she was driving around town, keeping all her business appointments, with a wrist so damaged that even she thought it needed to be x-rayed. By coincidence, I was on my way to her place. I withheld my dismay, agreed to pick her up at 4:30, and continued driving to her place to drop off some groceries, only to find her there when I arrived, getting a late lunch and trying to soothe her wrist with a bag of frozen peas.

When I asked why she was waiting to get it x-rayed, she said, "The doc who's buying Dorothy's house looked at it this morning and told me it's probably just a sprain." Though the wrist was quite swollen, she was continuing to take calls on her iPhone and messages on her iPad, which led me to wonder out loud if she intended to take them to the crematorium when the time comes. Her laughter at that moment assured me she was in better shape than her wrist, and capable of handling yet another appointment on her schedule, so I went home and worked on this report until she called, then I drove her to the emergency room at University Hospital.

Given the crowded waiting area, she didn't get cared for until five hours later, when an x-ray revealed she had broken her wrist, requiring a heavy and cumbersome splint from a few inches above her elbow to the first joint behind her fingertips. So, she's challenged now by anything that requires two working hands—like opening a jar, cutting a piece of meat, putting on a jacket, tying her shoes, or hooking her bra. But Jackie has a two-foot-long shoehorn and a bunch of other gadgets and gambits to get herself together and get around town. She's sensible enough, too, that she agreed to cancel an impending trip to California.

Never having broken my wrist, I had no idea how each of our hands depends on the other. Like intimate companions, they work in harmony, often without any conscious effort, to perform a countless array of tasks. Thus, the loss of one leaves the other hobbled, as I should have known just from my daily typing experience, watching both sets of fingers in concert in the process of striking the keys. How surprising that until now I never realized their interdependence, and neither did Jackie, who "never imagined that trying to do things with only one hand could be so time-consuming and exhausting."

I was about to say our surprise made me wonder what else we've taken for granted, but then remembered how troubled I've been this fall by what's going on (or not going on) in my head, or my brain, or my mind, or whatever it is that accounts for the perception and recollection of things. To put it bluntly, I'm troubled by forgetfulness—and not just by the sudden loss of a word that's long been part of my vocabulary, or my inability to remember the name of a person I've known for several years. That's small-time compared to the blackout of things I've read in a book or seen in a movie or experienced in daily life itself.

A few days before Christmas, for example, I opened the back door and found a festive bag on the doorknob, with tissue paper inside it containing an orange plastic gizmo shaped like a dog's head, with round black spots for eyes and a nose, but without any note to identify the point of the gift or the identity of the giver.

After a few minutes of inspecting the head, I saw that it could be opened by lifting its ears, which led me to suppose that someone had left it in hope of a charitable handout. But I had no idea whether it was an appeal for pet food, money, or some other kind of contribution. The minute Jackie arrived, I told her about it, and she burst into laughter, exclaiming, "Don't you remember?"—a query I've heard so often that it's now a seriocomic motif of our life together. In this case, I had forgotten a three-day summer jaunt up to northeast Iowa climaxed by a delightful picnic with my editor, Holly, who brought a bunch of fresh carrot and celery sticks neatly packed inside a child's plastic lunch box identical to the one that turned up on my back door. Not until Jackie jogged my memory with a few pointed queries did I remember the trip and the picnic and those carrot and celery sticks neatly packed inside an orange container, but for some reason I still don't recall anything about the plastic dog's head. A strange lapse, given the boldness of its cartoonlike face—a product of Ikea that had evidently delighted Jackie so much she must have asked Holly for the source of it, and Holly took the hint as an occasion for the surprise gift.

Pondering that lapse of memory, I'm inclined to suppose (or I'd like to suppose) that I didn't ever see the cartoonlike head at the picnic, perhaps because I was looking away when Holly opened the lunch box containing the carrot and celery sticks. But it's not the only time I've come up short in conversations with Jackie and others. A few weeks ago, in mid January, a neurologist at University Hospital asked me to recall a few examples of Jackie's behavior, for a study she's taking part in to test a drug that might delay the early symptoms of mild cognitive impairment. Given my own impairment, it seemed absurd for me to serve as an observer of Jackie's cognitive behavior, particularly in light of what happened when the neurologist asked me to recall a few incidents with Jackie that had happened just a few days before the interview. A simple enough query, it seemed, until I drew a blank, unable to recall any specific incidents. I was blocked, and only in a moment of willful self-distraction was I able to recall a few incidents. Compared to Jackie's exceptional memory of her past clients and their families, I sometimes forget people several days or weeks after being introduced. Which puts me in mind of Alan Berliner's brief *New York Times* op-doc, "56 Ways of Saying I Don't Remember."

If I'd always been forgetful, such lapses might not be troubling, but I remember when my memory of past conversations was so detailed that Kate spoke of me as being "like a tape recorder." Leading classroom discussions for thirty-five years always compelled me to remember the thread of question and response, in order to keep the give-and-take focused and fruitful from start to finish of each class. But now that I've been out of the classroom for eighteen years, I've lost the skill I once possessed, as well as my powers of recollection. "Use it or lose it" is now a more haunting maxim than in years past.

I wish it were just an injury, like Jackie's broken wrist, that would heal in the course of time, but there is no splint or other contraption to hold a failing memory in place. From time to time, in fact, I've wondered if I'm on my way to Alzheimer's or some other kind of dementia, especially after Jackie and I took a short course this fall titled "Is There a Brain Area for Fear?" Though the course didn't answer that question or mention anything about fear, it familiarized us with so many areas and parts of the brain whose impairment contributes to age-related cognitive problems that even the most fearless of our aged compatriots must have wondered about the odds of their becoming tongue-tied or demented. Or thought about friends and relatives who've experienced such problems, as I did when the brain researcher was talking about stroke-induced aphasia. I recalled a visit with my friend Bob, a stroke victim who lost his memory of names. When I visited him several months after the stroke, we had a conversation that was like a game of charades—he giving me clues about a famous person whose name he was trying to remember, I unable to come up with it, which led him to burst out in laughter, exclaiming, "You're stupider than I am." A week after the lecture that provoked the memory, I thought of it again, when Amy and Hannah came for a visit, in the midst of which Hannah received a call that her father-in-law (my counterpart) had suffered a stroke affecting his ability to speak. A week later, Jackie got the news that Stan had suffered a stroke. So, between the course and those coincidental reports, I couldn't stop imagining a brain problem in my future (or my present), even during the wonderful visit of Amy and Hannah, whose memories of things from their childhood here in Iowa City were so vivid they made me all the more aware of how little I remember from my past.

As if to reinforce that awareness, I've been reading Donald Hall's newly published *Essays after Eighty*, curious about his octogenarian experience, as well as his way of recalling and writing about it. Above all, he's very frank and self-deprecating about his recent physical mishaps, bodily infirmities, and mental lapses, but he never mentions memory problems. Indeed, his memory is so intact that he writes extensively and vividly about his past, much more so than about his octogenarian experience—recalling in specific detail not only the joys of his mid life marriage to the poet Jane Kenyon, but also his intense grief over her death from leukemia; reminiscing not only about his youthful travels abroad with his first wife, but also about his pleasurable childhood with grandparents and great-grandparents; writing not only about his lifelong attachment to Eagle Pond, his family home in New Hampshire, but also about his numerous books, public readings, and honors. Such a tour de force of recollection that I wondered how much of it might be the result of his keeping a journal. But in early childhood, where so many of his memories are lodged? His exceptional recall might also be explained in part by his acknowledgment that "for sixty years I have been writing my autobiography in book after book, poetry and prose." Though I cannot claim such a lifelong preoccupation, having written only four autobiographical works during the past twenty years, those chronicles of mine rarely sparked memories of childhood or such detailed memories of the past as his. So, Hall's compelling memory has made me even more concerned about my own.

In the face of such concerns, Jackie reminds me that I'm still able to recite some Shakespearean sonnets and other poems I memorized in graduate school, though I hasten to remind her that I memorized those poems during a time when my memory was unimpaired, and thus have always been able to call them up when they seem particularly relevant. Speaking of memories that have survived from my time in college, the one that lingers most of all is of the hi-fi rig with a full-size speaker that I put together during my sophomore year at Michigan, living for the first time in an apartment of my own. Immersing myself in Dvorak, Sibelius, Ravel, and Stravinsky was so thrilling, especially at high volume, that I took no heed of how the reverberations in such a confined space might damage my ears or how the damage might increase during the next fifteen years that I used that hi-fi system. There's nothing like self-inflicted damage to keep the memory of its origin in mind.

Though my hearing is beyond repair, a lunchtime conversation with my friend Nancy, a recently retired professor of business, led me to see that my memory might not be in such bad shape—that its lapses might not be the result of aging or mental impairment, but simply the byproduct of not being in the moment, or as Jackie might say, "of not paying attention." I realize that my mind is often somewhere else, whatever I'm doing, whether I'm alone or with others. But it never occurred to me that Nancy, who always seems to be in the moment, might be similarly inclined, until I was telling her about my forgetfulness and she surprised me by sharing a problem that she attributed to a longtime inclination to let her mind wander, even in the midst of things. Nancy's self-reflection led me to read a few pieces on memory, which revealed what I should have known all along—that memory of an experience is impaired if one is distracted or inattentive during the actual experience. By the same token, if one is paying attention, the memory of an experience will remain as vivid and detailed as my recollection of the afternoon last month when my oncologist told me in a very firm and assuring tone of voice that I'm unlikely to suffer a recurrence of the Hodgkin's lymphoma that beset me five years ago, but then advised me not to mistake that assurance for anything more than itself. Not only do I remember what he said, but I also recall looking at the shiny black pennyloafers he always wears. A whimsical bit of attire, like a signature, that put me in mind of the blue denim farmer's jacket that I often wore (with a shirt and tie) during my years of teaching at Iowa. Given how much I remember from that appointment with him, I've been making an effort to be in the moment, to keep myself focused on whomever I'm with, whatever is being said, and whatever is happening. The results have been so promising I'm grateful to Nancy for leading me to see how it might be possible to repair my memory (or the remnants of it), without benefit of a splint.

Yet I'm prone to relapse, as I did a few days ago at the end of watching *Still Alice*, the compelling movie whose detailed preoccupation with the gradual onset of Alzheimer's and memory loss in an accomplished academic should have made me hyperattentive. But my attention lagged in the midst of the final scene, leaving me unable to recall the last bit of dialogue between Alice and her daughter Lydia. Such a distressing lapse I wanted to scream for want of remembering. Though I retrieved the dialogue via Google, the memory of that relapse has made me even more attentive since then and more vigilant to be so. It's also made me more alert to how differently people react to memory loss. My former colleague Alan spoke of being "quite embarrassed" by it, whereas Don, a friend from the psych department, spoke of it in a seemingly dispassionate academic style as "age-related decreased memory ability," and my former colleague Oliver, with a twinkle in his eye, sought to console my distress about it by telling me how he forgot a word on his way to looking it up in the dictionary. And I consoled myself as usual with the realization that my ability to write about my memory lapses was evidence that I hadn't completely lost it.

In the course of such conversations, I've come to realize that my memory lapses often arise not only from inattentiveness, but also from an inability to recollect things speedily if I am in the midst of a conversation. Whenever Jackie mentions a past experience and I give her a blank look or an "I don't remember that," if she jogs my memory with a few reminders, then I'm usually able to recall the events in detail. In other words, I'm slow on the uptake, especially in the midst of an ongoing conversation, when I'm often so discombobulated by an inability to hear things as well as I'd like that recall is sometimes impossible. No wonder Jackie thinks I'm "much smarter in writing than in conversation," for writing gives me plenty of time to remember things that might not come to mind in the midst of a rapid verbal give-and-take. No wonder I'm tempted to be a hermit, spending my days at home with this chronicle.

Eighty-Two to Eighty-Three ✒

Teaching, Itching, Pondering Oaknoll

MARCH 2015 TO AUGUST 2015

Ever since retirement, I've avoided the classroom, at first burnt out by the demands of class preparation, office appointments, committee meetings, and batches of student writing, now estranged not only by eighteen years away from the academic grind, but also by my hearing problems and reports of classes rife with smartphones and laptops. Though I've declined invitations to teach at the senior center or visit a class in the nonfiction writing program, how could I refuse Jackie's young friend and fitness trainer Mia, especially after she told me she assigned my recent craft book in her writing course for sports management students? "Just one session," she assured me, "and the class meets for two hours, so there's time for in-class writing." Which meant I could plan a session preparing them to write, allow for writing time, then lead a discussion of their in-class writing—a familiar and useful routine. So how could I refuse?

No sooner did I accept than the worries began about everything I needed to plan, from a preclass reading assignment to the in-class writing assignment to passages and topics for the prewriting discussion. So many details to be taken care of that thoughts about Mia's course beset me even during a weekend with Jackie in New Orleans, six weeks before the class in late April.

Not even our engaging hosts, Jackie's daughter Mindy and her partner, Mary, distracted me from thinking about that course, nor did the Garden District, fine dining, or Kitty's Room, our amply furnished place at the Melrose Mansion. How strange, after forty-two years of teaching, to be as panicky as if I were preparing for my first class.

Performance anxiety, I now realize, is chronic and incurable, especially in persons who thrive on public approval, and who among us is indifferent to it? For the question that continued to echo in my head is, "Can I still rise to the occasion?" I did, thanks to several weeks of studying my little craft book and fussing over three different versions of a brief autobiographical piece, each version containing the same information, but each in a different style (one slangy, one formal, one literary and metaphorical), which I discussed with the class before asking them to produce two or three versions of a brief autobiographical piece, each one containing the same information but each in a different style. Samples of their in-class writing sparked a lively discussion of how changes in wording can produce striking changes in the sound of one's written voice, even when the informational content remains the same. I used this routine in years past with excellent reactions and was pleased that Mia's students were also impressed by it and by their own versatility in style-switching and role-playing.

What I didn't expect was the excitement of being in the class-room again, the give-and-take of discussion so engaging that my preclass anxiety gave way to the pleasure of witnessing students come to life in the process of analyzing and characterizing each others' writing variations. It's been so many years since I beheld such immediate learning, I had forgotten that special reward of teaching small discussion courses. A remembrance that made me grateful to Mia and her students, which in turn made me wonder why I retired at sixty-five. Why hadn't I continued for several more years?

A few days after the class, several students sent thank-you notes, encouraged no doubt by Mia but resonant with touching recollections of the day itself. And in the months since then, I've thought about it again, because of Jackie's occasional prodding—"Mia said your class went so well, you should think about offering a course at the senior center." But offering something for folks my age would make me nervous from start to finish. Anxiety such as that was rarely a problem during my forty-three years in the classroom, which leads me to surmise that aging has made me uncomfortable at the thought of being in the public eye. An alien notion for someone as sociable as Jackie, but an impulse that takes me back to my childhood shyness and to my wallflower days at high school dances.

In a quite different way, my current experience takes me back to childhood, given the dry skin itchiness of old age that's beset me the past several years, reminding me of an itchiness so many years ago that I was treated for several times at the Cleveland Clinic. Now as then, my arms and legs so itchy I scratched them raw all winter and spring. My scratching so persistent that Jackie, who rarely calls a doctor even when she's badly in need of one, said, "You've got to have someone take care of that." And I did, by consulting dermatologists at the University of Iowa. Two of them examined me from head to toe, each poring over my body with a small magnifying glass, so absorbed in their technical chatter about one spot or another—on my foot, my arms, and my back—that I felt like a clinical specimen, as indeed I was. The lesions I had produced by scratching the itchy spots led me to apologize for having done so. "No need to apologize," they said, almost in unison, "it's the itch-scratch syndrome"—my scratching authorized in a bit of clinical jargon. Diagnosing my condition as age-related, dry skin eczema, a distinctly different problem from the neurodermatitis of my childhood, they recommended skin moisturizers such as Aquaphilic and Cetaphil and provided me with a sheet of useful information about dry skin, detailing its appearance, its causes, its problems, its treatment, and so on.

The moisturizers and their advice helped quite a bit until Jackie and I headed off for a week on the coast of Maine in mid July, and I absentmindedly left the moisturizers at home. But it was so pleasurable and distracting to be on a schooner off Camden with our Rhode Island friends Bob and Jo Ann, then briefly in Brunswick where I had my first full-time teaching job at Bowdoin College more than fifty years ago, then in Rockland to see the portraits and landscapes of Andrew Wyeth, that I wasn't bothered much by the itching. When we returned home, I started using the moisturizers again, and the itchiness has subsided again. But in the midst of drafting this piece, I began to wonder if the dry skin, rather than being caused by advanced age, might be the result of my deficient thyroid, which also causes dry skin, and thus might be remedied by increasing my daily thyroid supplement. I asked my internist for a thyroid test and, after receiving the results, she reported that they showed an adequate amount of levothyroxine, which makes me wonder if I've been suffering from something more serious than age-related, dry skin eczema, such as age-related reality denial.

I wish it were possible to stop thinking about the itchiness, but at a local bistro recently with friends Hank and Mary Ann, both of them a few years older than I am, Mary Ann asked how I've been feeling lately. A polite question called for a polite upbeat reply, but I answered with a frank account of my itchy skin, mindless of whether she might be turned off by a self-pitying tale about it. Far from being turned off, Mary Ann held up an arm to show me her dry wrinkly skin and proclaimed her itchiness to be "so maddening I can't forget about it." Misery does, indeed, love company. And as if to provide an additional bit of confirmation, the next day at lunch our friend Dorothy asked what I'm writing about in this journal. My answer led her to announce that she too is afflicted with age-related dry skin itching, and her doctor prescribed triamcinolone, one of the anti-itch creams I'm using. I wonder how many others might tell me a similar story. Perhaps the signature of aging is itching—and instant testimonies about it.

Itching, though, was a minor digression during our time with Dorothy, for she had invited us to see her apartment in the new addition to Oaknoll. Such a bright, airy, and appealing place that Jackie and I were captivated by it. Jackie, the ever-cautious and discriminating realtor, exclaimed, "I could live here. I could live here with pleasure." And I echoed her like "Me Too" the chick, as we toured the new addition with its spacious and distinctive lounges, balconies, and walkways, as well as outdoor dining and sitting areas. All easily accessible, which made us feel that an apartment in this place would provide substantial living areas beyond the apartment itself. Which in turn made us reconsider our hesitations about Oaknoll. I agreed to contact the director and arrange for an informational tour, but couldn't help pondering our on-again, off-again reactions to the place.

Why is it that whenever we visit there, Jackie and I both come away with such favorable impressions we're inclined to sign up, but when we get back home and consider all the ramifications of living there we're more reluctant than before? I fret about having to pack up and leave this home of mine, where I've spent the best years of my life. And both of us are put off at the thought of having to eat so many meals in a collective dining room, as in the college dormitories of our past. Compelling enough reasons to give us pause, though we also feel compelled to keep Oaknoll in mind lest one or the other of us needs long-term care that's available in Iowa City only at Oaknoll. The ultimate push-pull situation, given an intense yearning to continue living as if one were ageless, while recognizing the illusoriness of such a desire. So, it's not surprising that we're torn and that Oaknoll is a leit-motif of this chronicle.

One other reason for my reluctance is that moving to Oaknoll would compel me to declutter this four-story house containing some forty-five years of accumulation. An awareness that's bedeviled Jackie ever since we took up with each other some fourteen years ago. Given her real-estate dealings with aged clients, she has a keen sense of how hard it is for them to declutter a home they've lived in for many years. She urges such clients to start a year or two before they intend to move out. Likewise, she's often suggested that I start with one room, or a half or corner of a room—"the sooner you start the easier it will be; the more you put it off, the harder it will be." A commonsense view of things that I should have heeded when she first made the suggestion. Given my repeated procrastination, Jackie recently told me, "You've got to get ready to leave," a resonant imperative fraught with the double-edged sense of "to leave." And she followed that imperative with another—"You should begin with the basement."

Nothing bears witness to the passing years quite like a basement, especially if you've been living above it for more than half your life, and it's large enough to hold all the things you no longer need or no longer use but can't bring yourself to part with. It's a memory bank of sorts, in remembrance of things past. How else to make sense of the dusty croquet set that Kate and I enjoyed when we first moved in, or my old badminton racquet leaning against the mallets under the work table where I've piled up the paint cans from days of yore? Or the foot locker next to the table with the ice-cream maker atop and the picnic basket overflowing with paper plates and cups? Or the crates of vinyl records—all those 33 rpms—side by side with the foot locker? Or the porcelain tubes from a garden sculpture, now cheek by jowl with the records? All together they create a trove of evocative stuff that always triggers memories whenever I walk by it on my way to the laundry room. But for Jackie, the stuff is just stuff, and there's so much of it that it's more like an obstacle course than a trip down memory lane. A mess she doesn't want to inherit when I kick the bucket, for she rightly assumes I'll kick it before she does.

A few days after Jackie's command to clean the basement, Amy called, wanting to visit; then by a happy coincidence Marshall called wanting to visit during the same week, along with my strapping grandson Owen, which led me to tell them about decluttering the basement, and they were happy to help. Before they arrived, the basement looked as if it were inhabited by the Collyer brothers: barely a pathway from one room to the next. After they left, it was more spacious than it's been in forty-five years. But after making an inspection tour, Jackie asked, "When do you plan to clear out the rest of the stuff?" Her query took me by surprise, given that our three days of sweeping, dusting, and carting things out had completely transformed the basement. Such a bizarre reaction, it seemed almost perverse until I realized that Jackie will only be content when the basement is empty, except for the washer and dryer in the laundry room. As if the house were ready for showing to prospective buyers. A realtor's dream, but for me an inescapable premonition of the end, as if I were on the verge of being carted away along with all the other refuse. No wonder that in Sweden, decluttering is known as "death cleaning."

That chilling thought led me to the backyard, after Amy and Marshall had left and the basement was (partly) decluttered. It was harvest time in the summer garden, the tomato plants pendulous with their red and orange fruit, framed at each end by purple eggplants, which roused my palate and brightened my thoughts with the realization that all I needed were the requisite cheeses in order to make an eggplant parmesan. A pleasure to savor in advance, layering up all the ingredients, topped by the grated parmesan, until I remembered that my gardening days, like the plants themselves, are numbered.

Eighty-Three ⦉

Distractions, "The Walk," a Cautionary Tale

AUGUST 2015 TO FEBRUARY 2016

The past several months have been quite distracting in many ways, so I'm writing this installment without having finished the one that precedes it, and without having the notes I ordinarily use to jog my memory. Distractions started with the summer campaigns, especially Bernie Sanders's populist promise of universal health care and Donald Trump's nativist promise of an anti-immigrant wall. By early fall, their working-class socio-economic appeals attracted large audiences, as did the fall and winter debates in both parties. The highly focused contest between Bernie and Hillary was very different from Trump's against the sixteen other Republicans, which made it difficult to ignore the evolving political psychodrama in both parties. Most of all, it was difficult to ignore the racism of Trump and the brutal fanaticism of his followers—their doings incessantly covered in newspapers and magazines, on the internet, radio, and TV. Jackie too has been distressed by Trump and his rabid crowds, so we rouse each other in a dialogue of competing news-bits: "Have you heard? Have you heard?"

When not tracking the debates and Trump, I've been distracted again by the stock market, thanks to its volatility the last several months—ten percent drops and bounce-backs, first from August through September, then again in January and February, each of which led me to sell in panic, then buy back in panic that I might miss the upswing. Such erratic behavior makes me wonder if I should put my money in a short-term investment-grade bond fund and leave it there at two percent interest, or even safer in a multi-year CD at two percent.

Our time up north in early September didn't do much to distract me from the market and Trump, for it didn't provide as much satisfaction as in years past, thanks to a marked decline in the frequency, length, and challenge of our hikes. We spent only a few days hiking this time, compared to our daily hikes before; none more than two or three miles, compared to four or five miles before; and most along level to moderate inclines, compared to steeper ups and downs before. Tangible evidence of aging bodies and limited energies that neither of us can ignore.

As if to reinforce that awareness, I came across an article in PLOS ONE focused on age-related changes such as ours, "Age-Related Variation in Health Status after 60," the conclusions of which noted the pivotal nature of octogenarian life: "Age eighty to eighty-five is a transitional period when major health changes take place. Until age eighty, most people do not have functional impairment or disability, despite the presence of chronic disorders."

Those telling observations and our experience up north clearly shaped our reactions to *The Walk*, a compelling reenactment of Philippe Petit's 1974 high-wire performance between the Twin Towers that we watched after returning to Iowa City. Though we'd seen a few static shots of Petit's feats on the wire, they barely anticipated the dizzying perspective of Robert Zemeckis's 3D film, 100 stories above the street. A perspective in which we remained for almost an hour, beholding Petit's stand-in not only walking back and forth on the wire again and again, but also gliding, dancing, kneeling, and lying on it. His every move was fraught with a greater likelihood of falling, given the increasing stress of his time on the high wire, in motion or not. We felt the stress in our panicky octogenarian nerves, even though we knew the outcome and knew that the film was a harmless reenactment. Yet we felt more tired at the end of the movie than we had at the end of our two- or three-mile walks.

Perhaps it would be more accurate to say we were emotionally drained, given such an edge-of-the-seat spectacle as Petit's "walk." Drained not just by the walk itself but also by everything preceding it: the high-energy, high-speed, high-risk scheming that enabled such an illegal venture atop the heavily guarded unfinished towers—a scheme that required Petit and his cohorts to hoist that high-wire cable to the top of the towers and affix it from one tower to the other in the span of a single evening. And before the movie depicts that hectic scheme, it bears witness to the development of Petit's acrobatic life from his youthful beginnings as a juggler, unicyclist, and would-be high-wire performer to the emergence of his consuming ambition (his death-defying coup, as he called it) to perform atop the towers.

But why have I discussed this movie at such length? In part, it's the combination of a vivid biopic and an arresting reenactment of an iconic event, each so distinctive and compelling in its own right as to defy a combination of them. More importantly, it displays one person's single-minded dedication to a lifelong ambition that is at once so creative and life-threatening as to be exceptionally paradoxical. An epitome, in its unusual way, of the risk and self-sacrifice that is inherent in any great lifetime achievement, whether it's Michelangelo's or Madame Curie's. High-wire performers are not thought of as belonging in such distinguished company, but Petit's exceptional performance is a reminder that greatness can emerge where we least expect it.

The memory of Petit's remarkable achievement buoyed me up during a life-threatening experience of my own, a few months after seeing the movie. It didn't involve even a hint of greatness on my part, but it does reflect the greatness of contemporary medical care in dealing with a crisis that might beset anyone in their eighties, given the various medical problems involved. So, the remainder of this piece is a detailed account of that crisis, intended not only as a cautionary tale, but also as a guide to surviving such an event and to reclaiming one's well-being thereafter.

My troubles began the night of the Iowa caucuses, when I stood outside in a cold rain, waiting in line for more than a half hour to enter the meeting room in an overcrowded little church, capable of holding no more than 300. Why didn't I leave when I saw all those people waiting to get in? Why did I stay two hours crowded with more than 600 others—a hothouse for colds—waiting to register my vote and hear the tally? Two days later I was beset with a harshly sore throat and the day after that with a "violent" cough, as my university internist described it. The remedies he prescribed did little to reduce the cough, which so disturbed my sleep and appetite that I lost twelve pounds the next eight days and noticed my left cheek sinking in, leaving my face visibly imbalanced. I urged Jackie to stay away lest she come down with the cough, as my internist had. Shortly before the cough had started, a malignant tumor was removed from the upper left-hand side of my chest, but the doctors assured me that it had nothing to do with the cough and that it was quiescent.

Day by day, I not only ate less and slept less than the day before it, but also felt so weak and helpless that Jackie later described me as having become "incredibly passive." After eight days of that violent cough, I called Amy to get her nursing advice, and she said, "You need to go to the emergency room right now, dad. You're in serious trouble. Get Jackie to drive you there. Don't try to drive yourself." I hadn't driven since the cough started. Fifteen minutes after talking with Amy, Jackie arrived and drove me to Mercy, the nearby local hospital, where I was diagnosed with atrial fibrillation, otherwise known as Afib, a dangerous condition in which the heart beats so rapidly and irregularly, it doesn't provide adequate blood flow to any of the organs, including itself.

The diagnosis surprised me, since I thought my problem was the debilitating cough. And it's a worrisome diagnosis, given its dangerous ramifications. As I later discovered, my age, heart disease, and previous heart attacks predisposed me to Afib. But I was then too weak and befogged to understand the interconnections. I hadn't even recognized my need for emergency care. The doctor's response to my surprise was a simple question: "Didn't you feel your heart beating very rapidly? It's known as tachycardia, and most people immediately feel the palpitations in their chest." But those sensations had been obscured by the violence and persistence of the cough. And the cough, together with my susceptibility to Afib, probably gave rise to it, which then led to other serious conditions, as I would learn in the days to follow.

After prescribing the blood thinner Eliquis to prevent strokes, my attending physician released me the following afternoon with a directive to contact my cardiologist and arrange for a heart checkup as soon as possible. The next Wednesday, an echocardiogram revealed I was not only in Afib but also had heart failure in the left ventricle. It was pumping blood at only fifty percent of normal, apparently because of a silent heart attack—the most shocking news of all—which made me wonder when the attack had taken place and whether it was the cough or the Afib that provoked it, or something else altogether. Neither my cardiologist nor additional tests could answer the question. Rather than looking back, she was looking forward, toward therapy, given a blood test that indicated my kidneys were worse than before, because of the heart problems.

At that moment it became clear I had a cascading set of troubles, one malady leading to another, until the whole batch of them might lead to endgame. My cardiologist focused her treatment plan on the heart problems, assuming that improved heart function and blood flow would lead to improved kidney and lung function. Her instructions included a list of prescriptions to control the heart rate, remove fluid in the lungs, and prevent stroke, as well as a follow-up blood test to check on the kidneys, and a few weeks later something called electrical cardioversion, otherwise known as shock treatment, to get the heart out of Afib and back to a normal rhythm. Plus "admission to university hospital if follow-up blood test and checkup show no improvement."

Subsequent tests revealed such a further decline that an urgent phone message directed me to the hospital for immediate admission. All those problems from a thoughtless night at the caucus subsequently led me to see that advanced age and chronic conditions had left no margin for careless behavior.

Being in the hospital was a relief at first, since I didn't have to cook for myself, didn't have to deal with the challenge of walking up and down stairs in my house, and didn't have to feel sheepish about spending every day in bed. Like a slacker, I wiled away the hours reading, surfing the internet, and watching TV coverage of the primaries. Looking back on my bedridden behavior, it's surprising that I didn't think to get up and walk the hospital corridors until my last two days in the hospital. Though I'm tempted to say that no one advised me to do so, I've long known from reading and previous experience how debilitating it can be to spend several days in bed. Pondering such a disconnect between my knowledge and behavior, I suppose that my brain was addled by inadequate blood flow. Another instance of Afib's insidious effects.

After a couple of days in the hospital, my initial sense of relief gradually gave way to increasing concern with the lack of immediate relief for my heart and the worsening of my kidneys, verging on the level when dialysis is needed. Persistently wakeful nights also troubled me. And I was worried about an upcoming procedure known as a transesophageal echocardiogram, in which a mini camera is thrust down one's throat to check the back of the heart to be sure no clots are there that could be shocked loose during cardioversion, and travel to the brain, thereby causing a stroke. That scary procedure turned out to be painless, and better still it quickly revealed there were no clots at the back of my heart.

Two days later, when I was being strapped into a framed rectangular bed with paddles on my chest for the cardioversion, I had a few moments of anxiety about the possibility of a shock-induced stroke. But the intravenous sedative put me out, and I woke to the report that my heart was back in normal rhythm, excellent news that led me to think all my other problems would quickly be solved, since they'd been caused by Afib. My kidneys would rebound, heart failure would be remedied, and energy would return. Even the cough would be cured, since it too had resulted from the inadequate blood flow of Afib. A veritable panacea, a quick and total fix.

Those illusions were dispelled during the next two days, when my kidneys showed no improvement and my weakness showed no signs of abating. So, even when my cardiologist released me after a week in the hospital, she said, "The blood test indicates your kidneys haven't improved, but we're worried that keeping you here will only make you weaker than you already are, and we're confident that over time the kidneys will rebound as you and your heart get stronger." Though delighted by the good news, that little phrase, "over time," dispelled the illusion of a quick fix, compelling me to realize it would take weeks or months for my heart, kidneys, and sense of well-being to rebound. And how could I have thought otherwise, when still so weak that a walk back and forth in the hospital corridor was exhausting? A far cry from our walks up north, and a galaxy away from Petit's wire-walking feats. But a walk of sorts nonetheless.

The first few days at home, I sometimes wished myself back in the hospital, free from the up and down of the stairways and the hassles of preparing low-salt meals tasty enough to be tolerable. My taste buds were beset by amiodarone, a heart-stabilizing drug with numerous side effects, one of which often made things taste metallic and another that made my favorite fresh fruits intolerable. Given those taste distortions, I couldn't eat more than two meals a day without getting queasy, which made me wonder whether those conditions would improve a week or two later as the dosage gradually decreased to the maintenance level. Surfing the web about amiodarone, I also discovered it to be the cause of my nightly sleep problems and a mild hand tremor. Five or six times a night I wakened, and returning to sleep came slowly, despite the sleep aid melatonin. Fragmented, disjointed, and abbreviated sleep left me weak and out of sorts, wondering when the various problems would diminish and my sense of well-being return. All of which is to say I continued to be impatient despite realizing the delusion of a quick fix. But impatience also spurred me to look for ways of improving things on my own, rather than relying entirely on the doctors.

The insidious effects of sleep loss led me to do an internet search using the phrase "remedies for sleep problems," and on WebMD.com I found a detailed discussion of natural remedies. Most notable was the advice to avoid illuminated screens, such as computers and TVs, well before bedtime, since they not only stimulate the eyes and activate the brain but also mimic the experience of flying through several time zones, as in jet lag. Compelling news to me, so I now shut down my computer and TV two hours before bedtime and spend the remaining time with restful, low-key reading. I also decided to extend my bedtime an hour (from 10–10:30 to 11–11:30), to be more sleepy when I hit the sack. And after two weeks on that revised pre-bedtime regimen, together with melatonin, my sleep is much improved, so I now wake up only once or twice a night to urinate and return to sleep much more quickly than before.

The hand tremors also led me to look for natural remedies, and the search turned up chamomile tea and valerian, both of them safe in and of themselves, but both of them liable to interact with my medications. I hope the natural remedy of improved sleep will also help to reduce the tremors. As for the other side effects of amiodarone—the metallic taste and the queasiness—they both gradually disappeared as the dose gradually decreased. By the end of the second week at home, when Jackie was in California, my appetite had improved enough to enjoy a scampi-like dinner of sautéed shrimp and thin spaghetti at a nearby restaurant with my friends Carrie, David, and Rebecca, whose hearty appetites left me hoping for even more improvement. Last, but not least, my kidneys have also rebounded—not to pre-Afib levels, but no longer verging on a need for dialysis.

Now, a month after returning home, my stamina has improved

enough that I'm walking again on the treadmill, gradually working up to my previous levels (1.5 miles in thirty minutes), a surprising turnaround from my time in the hospital. Even more reassuring is the rebound of my mind and will to survive, reflected in my research on amiodarone and its side effects.

Beyond such attempts to improve my well-being, the most surprising and satisfying result of the rebound is an ability to write more quickly and fluently than in recent months. Or as I told Holly, "The words come much more easily now than ever before." I was able to produce this piece in eleven days, and now have ideas for finishing the previous one, which I've been stalled on for almost seven months. Given the long delay in finishing that piece, I'm now inclined to think the silent heart attack might have taken place several months ago and thus have caused a decline in my mental ability and writing facility. The rebound has given me firsthand knowledge of what resilience involves and an equally strong awareness of what's required to maintain it. All of which is to say that I'm sleeping with one eye open.

And not just because of a cough that led to an almost total collapse, but also because of the malignant tumor on the upper left-hand side of my chest that was removed just a couple of days before onset of the cough. Though the surgical wound has completely healed, the scar is still visible, a reminder that I'm not really as well as I seem to be, that all those medical issues on my medical chart are latent dangers, capable of undoing me in several ways. A biopsy of that malignant tumor confirmed a prior needle biopsy, indicating the presence of non-Hodgkin's lymphoma. A confirmation of my oncologist's cautionary remark last year: "Though you've been free of Hodgkin's so long that it's not likely to return, there's no assurance of your being free from other forms of lymphoma or some other kind of cancer." In a similarly double-edged remark, he recently told me "the non-Hodgkin's cancerous cells are still so small there's presently no need to treat you," the wording of which clearly contains a warning that they might at any time grow larger and multiply.

In other words, I'm listening closely, heeding all the words and symptoms, more vigilant than ever before, lest I be lulled into the complacency that almost did me in.

Now, I mean to enjoy my present sense of well-being as much as possible as long as it lasts, without fussing any longer over the details of these past two months, except to note that my left cheek is filled out again and my face is back in balance, as am I. So, I'm off to start some eggplant, pepper, and tomato seeds for a bountiful summer garden. And then to celebrate the twentieth year of my Jeep Grand Cherokee, which survived a few serious problems of its own the past year, including the breakdown of its transmission, the weakening of its brakes, and the demise of its information panel. But now it's up and running again, as well as its owner.

Eighty-Three to Eighty-Four 🖋
Inattention, Overwork, Recovery

MARCH 2016 TO AUGUST 2016

It's early August, time to make something of all my notes for this installment. But the first thing that comes to mind is not in the notes, it's in my memory of what happened last night—or to be more exact what didn't happen. It was 5:30, the time Jackie shows up for dinner or calls telling me when she'll arrive. I was in the midst of slicing orange tomatoes, kalamata olives, yellow zucchini, and fresh mozzarella for an anti-pizza pizza, a concoction I devised with the help of Jackie, which she liked so much that she had a graphic designer produce a full-color two-page illustrated version of the recipe to share it with friends. Assuming she would arrive in time for dinner at 6:30, I put a pizza stone in the oven and preheated it to 475°. I also grated some parmesan cheese to sprinkle over the prebaked pizza. All the ingredients at hand, I was ready to coat a flour tortilla with pesto and then arrange small slices of tomato on its surface in the shape of a petalled flower. A recipe at odds with the thick crust, salty tomato sauce, and sea of rich cheese in most American pizzas, which led us to name it the anti-pizza pizza.

A half-hour later, Jackie hadn't yet been in touch, so I waited awhile longer, called her a couple of times without any answer, and left a message wondering when she'd arrive. Her absence and silence were so out of character I was befuddled and worried. The fact that Holly had emailed me earlier in the afternoon, mentioning her delight about lunch with "the redoubtable Jackie" just an hour or so before, increased my fears. Had something amiss transpired between lunch and dinnertime? By seven, I was on the verge of panic, haunted by the sudden deaths of two colleagues the past few weeks. I steeled myself and called the emergency rooms at both local hospitals, then their patient registries, but neither place had any record of her. A momentary sense of relief gave way to another dark thought—she might have collapsed or fallen at home. How else to make sense of my unacknowledged messages and her unanswered cell phone?

Driving across town to Jackie's place, I couldn't help thinking back to the day of Kate's sudden afternoon death, without any foreboding. Could Jackie be gone the same way? When I approached her house and saw her car in the drive, I expected the worst, as if life were being replayed in sudden death. Such an implausible recurrence I dismissed the thought—a product of my panicky, aged mind. But the panic recurred as I walked in the back door, expecting to find her passed out or dead. I was terrified as I called out her name. No sign of her in the kitchen or the living room, and no answer at first, so I walked to the basement stairway, called her name again, then heard a faint reply, "I'm down here." I didn't know what was up until she appeared at the foot of the steps and started walking up.

Her pale face made me think she might have suffered some kind of trauma. But when I inquired, she said, "I'm exhausted. I had a long day, with so many appointments I just got home." A surprising answer, given all my prior assumptions and expectations, which led me to ask why she hadn't called or answered my phone calls. "What phone calls?" was her reply—then, "there's nothing on my phone from you," which puzzled me even more. How could she not have heard my calls or had any record of them on her phone? (Inadvertently, it turns out, she'd blocked incoming calls from my cell number but didn't discover the problem until a week or so later.) Given Jackie's surprising reply, I told her everything about the past two hours—awaiting her arrival for dinner, calling her, calling the hospitals, calling her again. Which elicited another surprising reply—"Don't you remember my telling you last night that I wouldn't be coming for dinner this evening?" Her response dismayed me. A dreadful sign of my inattentiveness and memory lapses, which led me to vow that I'll definitely pay more attention from now on.

I wish it were the first time I made such a vow, but looking back through this chronicle via searches for "inattentiveness" and "pay attention," I found a long discussion of the problem in the last few pages of my entry for February 2015. Even without such an entry, I could hardly forget how often Jackie has asked me that question, "Don't you remember me telling you . . .?" Come to think of it, I now remember a time when Kate called out in the manner of a long-distance intercom voice—"Kate to Carl, Kate to Carl, are you there, are you there?" A witty wake-up call that made me aware of the problem as never before. How strange to be chided for an aggravating habit that I long associated with my brother rather than myself—a habit he developed during the years of his worldwide research on mother/infant bonding. Given that we've both got the distraction habit, I'd like to think it's an inherited trait and therefore unalterable. But the more I ponder the matter, the more evidence I gather that the habit I developed over the last forty years, in part from being preoccupied with essays and books I'm writing and in part from being increasingly hard of hearing, leads me to pay little or no attention to whatever is hard for me to hear. So, it's not surprising that Jackie often asks me, "Don't you remember?" I wonder how often that question arises in the world of other octogenarians.

How set we become in our ways as the years pile up. I've seen it not only in myself but also in Jackie and others. How else to account for her worrisome exhaustion the past several months? Though she's eighty-one, Jackie works full time during the work-week, consulting with colleagues and clients in the office or showing houses around town. Often she works more than eight hours, as if she were still young or only middle-aged, then after dinner, another hour or two of follow-up work in her home office. And a few hours as well on Saturday and Sunday. No wonder Jackie looks tired and pale when she comes for dinner during the week—a surprising condition for someone who takes such pride in her appearance. Her acknowledgment of fatigue tonight is also surprising for someone who takes pride in being unflappable and uncomplaining.

Now I can see why she told me back in April, "I think this is my last year doing real estate," an announcement I took with a grain of salt, until she added a bit later "I've not renewed my realtor's license, so I won't be able to continue after December." A hard decision for someone devoted to her clients and to the real-estate business—it seemed like a sure sign that Jackie was aware of her declining energy and continuing fatigue, which led me to think she would avoid a serious collapse like the one that beset me back in February. But ever since then, she's continued to work her usual demanding schedule, which contributed to my panic about her dinnertime absence.

On the other hand, in early July she was very calm and swift in responding to the costly results of a violent overnight storm—completely in keeping with Holly's description of her as "the redoubtable Jackie." She called me the next morning in a matter-of-fact voice to report that the seventy-five-foot sycamore tree in front of her house had been blown down in the storm, destroying her car, filling her front yard and her driveway as well as her neighbor's drive with its downed limbs, and that her insurance would cover only a fraction of the costs for removal of the tree and for a new car. Then she added, "It came just inches from destroying my house, so I'm grateful that it's only the car." Not only had she put her losses in perspective, but she had already arranged an interim car rental, talked with arborists about removing the tree, and contacted a specialist to deal with a large swarm of bees whose hive had been damaged by the falling tree. Later that day she was back at work; the next day she put in a full eight hours with colleagues and clients; a week later, she had bought a new car. The redoubtable Jackie indeed!

Which reminds me of an evening in early April when Jackie and I were watching the final four, she sitting on the floor, leaning her back against my legs. A comfortable arrangement until my sudden need for a visit to the bathroom led me to stand up quickly, lift my right leg over her head, lose balance on my left leg, and crash down on my right leg, in an attempt to avoid falling on her. A sharp pain struck the back of my right knee, as if I might have broken something, but then it was gone a few seconds later. But Jackie, I noticed, was silent, sitting there in pain and distress, a tear running down her cheek. The bottom of my shoe had scraped the inside of her ankle and scratched the surface of her skin. I apologized, gave her a hug, and hustled to the bathroom for a washcloth to cleanse her bruise, as well as an antibacterial ointment and Band-Aid to protect it. Though I was upset with myself for not warning her in advance, Jackie was quick to make light of the matter. If I could maintain such composure, my blood pressure might not be so erratic. But years of living with myself have convinced me that you can't teach an old dog new tricks. That maxim has helped me realize that fretting about one's erratic pressure—fretting too much about anything—can exacerbate the problem, as in a feedback loop. Now at last my blood pressure seems to be well controlled, no doubt because of my continued recovery from all the traumas of February. Recovery too can nurture itself, as in a feedback loop.

Thanks to having more energy than before, I've been able to tend and maintain a productive summer garden of eggplants, peppers, Swiss chard, tomatoes, and zucchini—hand-weeding the plot and cultivating the soil with a one-wheel plow. Sometimes I work two or three hours in the garden without any fatigue, a surprising turn of events given that I was so weak back in April, it was all I could do to plant a row of radish seeds. My mental energy has also improved, as I discovered from doing several hour-long interviews about the origin and development of Iowa's Nonfiction Writing Program for the University Library's "Memory and Knowledge Project." And I'm buoyed by the University of Iowa Press having made an unsolicited offer to publish this chronicle, with a word limit sufficient to cover another three or four years of installments. Now all I need is another three or four years of life to fulfill the contract.

Enough time also to declutter, downsize, and move to a smaller, more manageable home or to an apartment at Oaknoll. Though I've discussed the move with Jackie and my children, I've done very little about it beyond having a physical and cognitive checkup to make sure I'm qualified for Oaknoll. Jackie continues to be worried about the likelihood of my dying first and thus leaving her with a houseful of possessions and documents, without a plan for disposing of them, short of the dump. She keeps urging me to spend a couple of hours a day getting rid of superfluous things in the attic, the bedrooms, and so on, reminding me how long it will take to reduce all the stuff I've accumulated during forty-six years of living in this place. And reminding me again that the house will need to be completely empty when I move out and turn it over to the National Trust for Historic Preservation. Compelling imperatives, but so intimidating and depressing I've not done anything more than the basement. A few days ago, in fact, I couldn't help asking Jackie, "Why do you get to continue living in your home, while I have to move out of mine?" I knew the answer, of course, for her place is much smaller and more manageable than mine. "It isn't fair," she said, "I know it isn't fair." Luckily, a late August visit from Amy and Hannah made it feel more bearable and doable than I imagined. They flew in from California for a five-day visit and promised to return as many times as needed to declutter the house, just as Marshall had promised when he visited back in June. Not knowing how to proceed, I took an idea from my friend Jean, who asked each of her children to make a list of the furniture, artwork, and other possessions they wanted in advance of her move into Oaknoll—a far better system than trying to figure things out on one's own. Not content to rely only on lists, Amy and Hannah took iPhone shots of everything in every room on all four floors of the house. Now, I assume, they know what it means to do an inventory.

I also invited them to survey my library, choosing books they'd like, which led them to box up several cartons they'll take back to California the next time they drive here. The book-choosing was a bittersweet affair, beginning with Hannah finding a numbered first edition of Wallace Stevens' collected poems, which took me back to my student days in Ann Arbor, when Stevens was my literary idol and the book itself my bible. Now covered with years of dust from my neglect, it was a silent rebuke, so how could I cling to it? It wasn't much easier a day or so later when Amy, an ailurophile, discovered *Old Possum's Book of Practical Cats* and proceeded to recite the poems, book in hand. But then again, even as it was sad to let go of such things, it was a pleasure to behold my daughters taking such visible and audible joy in the possession of them. Gifts for the giver.

A day later, more accustomed to letting go, I took them to a pie safe in my bedroom, containing not only my clothes but a trove of Kate's sewing things—spools of thread, a small loom I'd given her for a birthday, a quilt in progress, and three large bundles of beautifully patterned material from our trips to Kauai. And then I saw her again in the Kapaia Stitchery, a swath of fabric in hand. A poignant memory sweetened by Hannah's sudden outburst, "I'll make you an aloha shirt from this one," holding it up in her hand. Then a few other finds: two hand-embroidered silk handkerchiefs—alternating dragons and flowers—from our month in China, and a framed bit of needlework from Kate's childhood—"My Name is Kate Franks"—now sitting on the dresser beside my bed. Everything bringing back her devotion to the arts of needle and thread.

The afternoon before Amy and Hannah headed back to California, I enjoyed our discoveries and their spontaneous reactions so much it was disarming to recall that just a few days before, when I asked them to make their want-lists, the whole thing felt a bit creepy and sad, as if I were hastening my own demise or witnessing an after-death division of my possessions. A black comedy of sorts, especially when Hannah exclaimed, "I want those two Achepohls," and Amy then declared, "I want the couch; I've wanted it for years." Oh yes, I remember Hannah voicing her sadness about "taking this beautiful place apart," so touching a phrase I won't forget it. But as the days passed, I could, after all, so easily bear it that letting go has come to seem like a most delicious thing. Now, as never before, I'm coming to understand the yin and yang of letting-go.

In mid July, I also beheld something that made me think about the yin and yang of things, thanks to awakening a few minutes before six, when it seemed a bit dark for that time of day. I went to the screened-in porch at the back of the house to see what was up on the east side, and there was confronted by a red sky, a spectacle I'd never seen before. I remembered seeing a red-streaked sunrise twenty years ago when I was keeping a daily weather journal, but never an all-red one like this. I ran to my bedroom on the south side, pulled open the wooden blinds, and there it was again, that dark red sky—which put me in mind of the adage, "Red sky in the morning, sailors take warning." I always thought it signified one of those red-streaked skies I'd seen before, whose streaks always began to fade almost as soon as they appeared. But this time the red was so pervasive and persistent that it made me wonder if something sinister could be involved, like a silent attack upon the air itself, like chemical warfare in the upper atmosphere. Was it the real thing or my aged imagination gone wild? I ran to the back porch again, looking for confirmation one way or another—still solid red. Such a weird and persistent spectacle that I ran to the front of the house, pulled open the front door, and there, thank god, it was all gray. And, surprisingly, all gray when I made a quick check again on the back porch. The red all gone, just like that, not a trace of it in the sky.

Eighty-Four 🖋

Decrepitude, Wisdom, Shingles, Downsizing

Many moons ago in an undergraduate English course, I first encountered "After Long Silence," Yeats's dramatic poem about love, art, age, and wisdom. But I was too young to get it. A single sentence in eight rhymed lines, it seemed a strange way to speak with a loved one after years apart—also strange to propose that they talk at length about "the supreme theme of Art and Song," by which he meant love, as reflected in drafts of the poem. But why such a high-flown way of referring to love, as if the word itself were not resonant enough? Then as if to compound the riddle, he followed that phrase with "Bodily decrepitude is wisdom." A memorable aphorism but irritating in its suggestion that the debilities of old age are the sine qua non for wisdom about the nature of love, as if youthful well-being were at odds with such understanding.

Now, sixty-five years later, I can see how "bodily decrepitude" might be a source of wisdom. But I don't mean to claim it for myself, nor to suggest that my body is decrepit. Indeed, my physical appearance continues to belie my age and numerous health issues, tempting me to consider myself an enigma of sorts, especially when doing a mile and a half on the treadmill in thirty minutes. But I'm sometimes given to such foolish behavior that there's no risk of self-delusion, as when I ignored Yeats's epigram last September at the end of a pleasurable week with Jackie in Grand Marais, and defied a doctor's imperative: "Don't push or strain on the toilet." Thirty years ago, when my cardiologist made that command after my heart bypass surgery, I obeyed it religiously. But the passing of time led me to ignore that wisdom. And the more I got away with it, the more I ignored it, until that Sunday morning.

The consequences were not immediate. But a few hours later, on the way to lunch, a small protuberance began to form an inch or two above my navel, and it soon became enlarged and painful, so I asked Jackie to drive me to the local hospital. The emergency room doctor told me to lie down on an examining table, where he felt the bulge and the surrounding area, asked about the severity of the pain and how far it extended beyond the protuberance, and then announced, "You have an abdominal hernia. Probably a bit of fat or muscle protruding through your abdominal wall. Not surprising for a person your age." The opening, he surmised, resulted from the weakening of a suture after the heart bypass surgery thirty years ago. Having made his diagnosis, he asked the question that triggered my dismay: "Did you strain yourself this morning, lifting something heavy, or pushing on the toilet?" A question that reminded me of that cardiac surgeon's command—and of Yeats's epigram. The minute I started to answer, the doctor swiftly brought both of his hands down on the bulge, pushing the protrusion back into place and the pain into memory. A dramatic intervention that I was surprised to learn is a standard procedure known as a reduction. Then it was time for some amiable conversation about the doctor's life in Jerusalem and his intermittent service at this far-flung little hospital. So, after all, I was delighted by the result of my disobedience, and wished that all my problems might be solved in such a quick and painless way. That wish reminded me of an ambulance ride ten years ago to the Mayo Clinic for life-saving heart surgery after a heart attack in Red Wing, the remembrance of which inspired a little poem—an anniversary poem of sorts:

AMBULANCE

How fast it goes from here to there,
when something precious needs repair:
your head, your heart, or other parts
that aren't in stock at super-marts.

Back home again, I attended a dispiriting memorial service for an admirable colleague. It sounded more like a professional resume than a memory of the person himself, a memorial service that made me think I'd just as soon have no memorial. Now I know why Kate's mother prepared a two-page set of directions for her funeral. My only request is that Jackie and my children enjoy a trip to Kauai on my tab, scatter my ashes in Hanalei Bay, where I scattered Kate's ashes, and thereby make me one with the sea and the sand of all my joyous times there, now long past.

I'd also be delighted if a few of my books live on in the hands and minds of others—a hope that came to mind thanks to an email from a fellow octogenarian, a former academic dean and scientific researcher, telling me how much he enjoyed my book about retirement. I offered to send him a copy of this work-in-progress, inviting his reactions and suggestions. He read it and responded by noting how little I've written about falling, whereas he's preoccupied with the fear of it, after slipping on the ice and breaking an ankle, as well as falling from his mountain bike and separating one of his shoulders. I resisted the urge to tell him how cautious I am, as is Jackie, when walking up and down the stairs, but the next day I ran up them, eager to watch the end of a football game on TV, and fell on the final step. Now I know why they always ask, "Have you had any falls lately?" Oh, that bodily decrepitude were a guarantee of wisdom.

Wisdom was also in short supply during the presidential campaign last fall. Its opposite so pervaded Trump's campaign—his lies, his tweets, his grandiose promises, his racism, sexism, and all-consuming narcissism—that he roused my apprehension more than any presidential candidate in the past sixty years. His grandiose slogan, incessant lies, and unstoppable tweets are so aggravating they provoked me to write my first ever political poem.

MAKING AMERICA GREAT AGAIN

First we lie, then we tweet,
The surest way to spread deceit,
Then we lie and tweet some more
Until we're greater than before.

The stock market was also disturbing—share prices so high, it seemed an October correction might be in the offing, so I sold almost all the holdings in my IRA in late September at very favorable prices. Though I breathed a sigh of relief at being ninety-seven percent in cash, the question of when to buy back into the market soon began to nag me, for I worried about losing potential gains from subsequent bounce-backs. In other words, I wanted to have it both ways, as if I were a master of market timing. Not until November, given the big increase after Trump's election, did the time seem right to get back in, but I chose much safer holdings than before. As a result, I ended the year with frayed nerves and an eleven percent gain, slightly better than the S&P 500. But from now on, I hope to avoid the stresses of market timing by holding only value stocks and holding on to them come what may.

The stress of maintaining a large old home also got to me last fall. Long a sanctuary and source of pleasurable gardening, it had become a daily reminder of rooms to be cleaned, clutter to be removed, books, clothes, cooking gear, and furniture to be sorted and given away, trash to be recycled, porches, windows, and overhangs to be painted, borders and beds to be weeded, and the increasing deer herd to be dispelled. All of which led me to tell Jackie in October that I want to move to a less burdensome place. She concurred with my interest in moving, for she'd been nudging me toward a smaller and more manageable house the past year or two. I'd long known she was right, but knowing is one thing, while facing and accepting the inevitable is another. For one cannot contemplate downsizing without realizing that it leads to the ultimate downsizing to a coffin or crematory urn. A definitive reminder that "you can't take it with you."

Once I made the decision to move, Jackie put me to work decluttering—garden books and antique canning jars to Holly; Kate's remaining clothes and old tablecloths to local charities; my ill-fitting but still wearable clothes to local charities; surplus cooking gear boxed up for Marshall; rusted canning pots, canned pickles from years past, and pieces of an old garden sculpture to the city dump. Throughout the house and around town, it was a nostalgic busyness that diverted me every day, until I was beset by shingles in mid October.

I didn't remember myself having chicken pox, but I remembered my brother's bout of it. Surprising to realize that I too had the pox, and thus was vulnerable to shingles, given my age and compromised immune system from lymphoma and chemotherapy. Had I gotten the shingles vaccine several years ago, before chemo weakened my immune system, I might have avoided it. But the vaccine can cause shingles in persons with weak immune systems like mine. Though I'd long heard about shingles, I never realized the damage it can inflict on nearby parts of one's body, until the rash and infection that first showed up on the inside of my left buttock and bedeviled everything nearby. So, from mid October to late December, I was beset by a series of pesky medical problems exemplifying the blunt view of my friend Stan that "something's always going wrong in your eighties."

While I was bemoaning the shingles, my oldest and dearest friend, Bob, was in the hospital for two weeks, beset by such severe medical problems he lived only a week after returning home. When his wife, Jo Ann, called to tell me about the lengthy hospitalization, I couldn't fathom it, for he'd been emailing me most of the fall about Iowa's football games, except for a few weeks in November. How could he be on the verge of dying, I wondered, but Jo Ann's reply—"he's not had good medical care the past few years"—was so puzzling and dismaying I chose not to aggrieve her with any other questions. I sent Bob an email, briefly about Iowa's football team, mostly about our wonderful times together and how he'd inspired me over the years, to which he replied, "We did a lot of great things together, my friend." A moving response, especially its stoic sense of finality and exceptional generosity. For though we were longtime friends from our years together in graduate school and collaborated on several textbooks over the next fifty years, Bob did so many great things on his own in literary criticism, theory, and professional reform that I often considered him as much a mentor as a colleague, a consummate guide as well as a loyal friend. The house I live in I bought from him, a way of reading I learned from him, and the joys of writing I shared with him. *Ave atque vale.*

In the wake of Bob's death, I had mixed feelings about leaving this former home of his, but the reality of his death reminded me of my own limits, as did the gentle proddings of Jackie. When she told me about an attractive place a mile or two out of town, I agreed to give it a look. She explained that it was in a neighborhood of zero-lot-line houses, in other words, pairs of side-by-side houses joined by a common wall. Jackie led me through the house, as if I were a client, pointing out all the features in its 2,400 square feet of living space—an up-to-date kitchen, living-dining area with vaulted ceiling, a bedroom on the main floor that would enable me to live on one level if need be, three other bedrooms and baths, as well as a large family room with a fireplace and walk-out below. One-third more living space than I have on the two main floors of my old home. I couldn't at first imagine what to do with it all, until it occurred to me that I might not have to do any more decluttering—I could take it all with me. Especially with extra space in the large garage, which was especially alluring, because my nineteenth-century home doesn't have one, and I've never been inclined to build one in the very limited space at the end of the driveway.

How strange to think I wouldn't be downsizing; I'd be upsizing. And Jackie, the muse of downsizing, didn't raise any objections. Far from it. She said at one point, "You'll have room for more of your books, and I'll have space for a room of my own." Those alluring possibilities led Jackie to measure the dimensions of all the rooms, considering where to place all my furniture and artwork—playing house as if we were starting life anew. And I was delighted by the prospects of not being burdened with gardening or deer, thanks to a yard consisting of a very small patch of grass behind the house, backed by a high metal fence. To each of us our own dream of a new old age. Oh yes, I wished the place had an attached screened-in porch like the one on our friend Mary's place a few doors away, also a fireplace in the living room, as at Mary's, and a handsome wood patio in back, partly shaded by a lovely tree, as at another nearby house. There is, after all, no end of wishing when a new life is on the horizon.

Reality set in when our inspector reported that retaining walls at the side and back of the house needed to be rebuilt, then contractors estimated ten to twelve thousand for rebuilding them, and the homeowner refused to make adjustments for them. The potential expense of those retaining walls led me to think about all the other costs associated with buying and moving into that house—and not just in dollars and cents but also in physical and psychological terms. More by far than I was willing to spend, since it was so inexpensive to stay put in my cumbersome old home—all paid up and donated to the National Trust for Historic Preservation, leaving me responsible only for home insurance and upkeep. Buying the new place, by contrast, would involve not only an expensive and burdensome move, but also an increase in my living expenses of almost two thousand a month. So, I decided to stay in my longtime home as long as possible. That's how my former department chair did it, and he seemed perfectly at ease when I visited him a few months before he died at his home.

To celebrate that decision, I made one of my favorite and simplest dishes—a one-pound pork tenderloin, spiced with herbs of provence, garlic powder, salt, and pepper, then rolled in olive oil before being seared on all four sides, five minutes a side, in a grill pan that yields medium rare meat. It is exceptionally tender, low-fat, and tasty. I paired the tenderloin with another of my favorite and simple dishes—wild rice mixed with diced sautéed mushrooms and diced scallions. I served the two with a perfect companion requiring no preparation at all—a bowl of commercially made unsweetened applesauce. All of which affirmed the joys of simplicity—in cooking and in staying put.

While I had been going through the pros and cons of moving and staying put, Jackie was going through a challenging time of her own. She was still working 24/7, as if she were sixty-one rather than eighty-one—sometimes so fatigued from a full day of appointments that she flopped down on the couch for a pre-dinner rest. Even when she didn't take to the couch, she often spoke of her exhausting days—unusual behavior for someone inclined to keep smiling even in the midst of pain. But having seen all the work she did not only in showing me that prospective house, but also in acquiring an inspector to examine it, contractors to bid on upgrading it, and a loan officer for financing it, I understood why she was exhausted and why she'd chosen to retire.

Jackie's impending retirement was troubling her, given the nagging questions of what to do next, of how to make something purposeful and satisfying of a work-free life—a double bind that was itself exhausting. When I mentioned the likelihood of toasts and tributes at the annual party of her realty firm, Jackie said, "I don't want any of that"—as if one could refuse. Not surprising from someone as self-deprecating as she. But when the time came and the tributes resounded, Jackie rose to the occasion with such a warm response it was clear she'd been deeply moved by the accolades of her colleagues. And the tributes continued—in the local newspaper, on Facebook, via email, letters, and cards—so many that her determination to answer all of them became another burden. But not so much she didn't enjoy a wry post acknowledging that "Jackie's done a lot of good things, but she's no saint."

Early in January, Jackie and I took a trip down memory lane, when Art Garfunkel came to town for a concert. Now seventy-six, he's a faint semblance of his former self, his voice no longer up to the music, because of vocal paresis he suffered several years ago, which made me wonder why anyone so strained and aged would persist in the burdens of touring, especially when he's well off from his incredible success. All in all, it seemed more like a valedictory than a performance, especially his recollections of Paul Simon and others from his past, as well as his reading of poems he'd written years before. As if he wanted to have the last word, when none of us, after all, can have it, given the words of those who succeed us.

The beginning of Trump's presidency at the end of January also made me think about the power and durability of one's words, thanks to the manic flurry of directives he signed during his first week in office. A craven rush of them that aggravated Jackie and me with the incessant flow of worrisome news—she hooked to her iPad, I to my MacBook—especially after his outrageous immigration ban. Several times during the first week, I vowed not to read anymore about Trump, not even a column headline, and urged Jackie to do the same. But neither of us could resist, which led me to read an article in the *Times* about the very same problem besetting millions of other Americans. Even the need to finish this piece by early February couldn't keep me focused on it, given the irrepressible urge to keep track of new outrages, which left me feeling that I'll never be at ease as long as he's in office.

But the painful recurrence of my hernia a couple of nights before the end of January distracted me from thinking about Trump. When the protuberance began to arise in the midst of watching CNN news, I remembered how it had once reduced after lying on my back in the emergency room. So, I went to bed, lay on my back, felt a strange sensation in the area of the hernia some forty minutes later, and the protuberance and the pain were gone. The next morning, I sent an email to my internist about the hernia episode, and two days later she examined the site of it. Though noting a slight protrusion, she reminded me that I have three risk factors against surgery—coronary artery disease, chronic kidney disease, and atrial fibrillation. So, my six-month report ends much as it began, with the continuing risk of a hernia I hope to reduce by reducing both my weight and any strenuous activity that might provoke it. A downsizing of sorts in hopes of more trouble-free years. Bodily decrepitude is wisdom.

Eighty-Four to Eighty-Five 🖋

Resilience, Reunions, Brotherly Loss

FEBRUARY 2017 TO AUGUST 2017

Several months ago, my former colleague Gene advised me "to be happy in the knowledge that we appear to have another spring and summer." A gentle reminder that being alive in one's mid eighties is a cause for celebration, even when the mental lapses that accompany old age result in an embarrassing mistake—like the moment after an enjoyable lunch with Jackie, Don, and Marcia, when I walked into a women's restroom for the first time in my life and didn't realize the error, thinking that the absence of urinals was the mark of an upscale hotel or a unisex restroom, until Don set me straight. But aside from that comedy of errors, the past ten months have been free of such mental lapses and free of serious medical problems. I'm knocking on wood, hoping to keep my well-being intact.

Also, I'm hoping the decision to stay in my old home continues to work as well as it has the past several months. After deciding to stay put, I discovered that gerontologists, social workers, and occupational therapists refer to it as "aging in place," a strange locution that doesn't suggest the various reasons for continuing to live in the home of one's choice and the complications involved in doing so. Especially when doing so involves an eighty-five-year-old in a four-story, 120-year-old house on a three-quarter-acre lot, an outlandish situation, given all those stairs to traverse several times a day, as well as all that land to maintain, not to mention all the hassles of an older home. But its glowing wood interior and its tall windows brighten my spirit, and I continue to thrive on the built-in cardio exercise of the stairs and the sloping backyard, which also help to keep my hips and knees limber. Fifteen years ago, my knees ached so much I consulted an orthopedic surgeon, whose exam and x-ray indicated moderate osteoarthritis. His recommended treatment: lose ten or fifteen pounds, exercise regularly, and take arthritis-strength Tylenol to relieve the pain. Following that regimen has enabled me to avoid surgery, and I no longer need the Tylenol.

Meanwhile, Jackie continues to be trouble-free. She still has no long-term medical conditions and has taken no long-term medications during our thirteen years together, a blessed state of well-being that enables her to fill her days with a hectic run of activities. A bout of fatigue and a summer cold last month led her to realize that she "wasn't meant to be Perle Mesta." Given her exuberant appetite for experience, that's a small price to pay. All of which is to say I admire—and envy—her remarkable constitution.

More admirable, though, is Jackie's resilient spirit, a quality that might be the most fundamental aspect of successful aging. Advanced age inevitably involves mental, physical, and existential losses that require a continuing ability to adapt, which is the sine qua non of endurance. I'm thinking, for example, of how swiftly Jackie adapted to retirement last December. Whereas I maintained an office in the department for two years, Jackie moved out of hers the day of her retirement and turned her attention to a new project—creating a small weekly salon to promote friendship among a changing group of women, unknown to each other but with similar interests. The swiftness of her transition from realtor to salonièrre surprised me at first, given how fondly she's often spoken of her clients as friends or family. I was also surprised by the substantial difference between negotiating the complexities of a real-estate transaction and preparing a weekly guest list and menu for the salon. But she could not have launched such an artful and sociable activity without knowing hundreds of women from her forty years as a realtor, nor could the salon have succeeded without the lively and generous personality that brightened her years as a realtor. At the heart of resilience is an upbeat spirit.

After writing that paragraph, I wondered how things in the garden had adapted to last night's raucous thunderstorm and was delighted to see all but one of the top-heavy sunflowers still upright, despite the heavy rain and wind. Most striking, though, was a sunflower whose stalk was bent downward, its top, four feet away, already bending up from the ground and reaching toward the sun. An epitome of resilience under the most challenging conditions—still inclined to bloom, come what may. The image put me in mind of my first wife, Meredith, whom I saw a couple of months ago for the first time in several years. Now crippled by osteoporosis and scoliosis, her body so bent that walking seems tortuous even with a walker, yet she gets around with a smile, her memory as quick, her mind as sharp as when we met sixty-five years ago.

I'm on an associative ramble, and Meredith's indomitable spirit reminds me that when she and I first met, my brother was recovering from the bout of polio he suffered as a medical student. The affliction impaired his right shoulder and arm, but he never complained about the loss of motility or the compensatory movements of his other arm that gradually left him so weakened on both sides he was only able to clothe himself with great difficulty. Despite those adversities, he went on to become an eminent neonatologist and researcher who transformed the care of newborn children and their mothers throughout the world.

Compared to such exemplars, my doings are trivial. Like buying a long-necked canister vacuum in early February, to clean this high-ceilinged house. Its neck long enough to reach into corners, under furniture, up and down radiators, up and down walls, up and down stairs, the vacuum is a user-friendly machine that has made me feel younger and more in charge of things than I have in years. Too bad the same can't be said of the morning exercises I started in early April at the suggestion of my friend Stan, to strengthen my abdomen and keep the hernia reduced. Though the exercises have helped those weak spots, they often remind me of my creaky joints. And the same goes for the large annual flower bed I created in the 44' × 22' space that used to be my main vegetable plot. Now it's a colorful array of zinnias and sunflowers planted in May, but I also feel keenly the increasing challenge of keeping it weeded, cultivated, and watered.

The best thing I did in the backyard was to hire Isabella, a sophomore here at the university, star center on the womens' soccer team, and self-effacing perfectionist who's been weeding and tending things since mid May. Thanks to her, the yard now looks better than it has in years. The hosta beds are restored, the overgrown raspberry bed reclaimed, the brick walkway behind the patio scraped clean and reset, and Kate's sixty-foot perennial bed fully weeded after two years of neglect. Yardwork I once did on my own in the ordinary course of things, but never so well as she. Now, except for tending my new flower bed and a few tomato and pepper plants, I've joined the ranks of gardeners who delegate their gardening to others.

Ah youth! The youth of others is not just an aid to aging in place, but also a source of stimulation, pleasure, and hope for the future, which I experienced a couple of times back in March. First, on an afternoon in Iowa City, when my granddaughter Kathleen came to town at the invitation of Iowa's African Studies program to give a very informative talk on land rights, land distribution, and political violence in Kenya. A compelling presentation from start to finish, especially considering that she spoke at length without a text and then responded to a wide range of questions. She's thirty-one, just a year older than I was during my first year at Iowa, but she's far more poised and articulate than I ever was, both in lecture mode and discussion. And far more in touch with the harsh realities of the world, given her extensive research in Kenya, Ghana, and Malawi.

A few weeks later in Charleston, Jackie and I were captivated by her grandson Elvin, who piloted his hand-built drone through acrobatical ups and downs over so large an area that it was sometimes visible only to him through his binocular-like goggles, until it came back into sight when he brought it down to land on a nearby strip of grass—without a wobble. Control panel in hand, piloting his craft, Elvin reminded me of the days when I sped my Lionel train around the tracks of the layout my brother and I put together some eighty years ago. But we could not have built or piloted a craft like Elvin's drone—evidence of his fitness for the engineering career of his choice.

I didn't expect a striking performance or wholly joyous occasion when I flew to California in early June for my brother Marshall's ninetieth birthday. Though I booked the flight in early April and looked forward to seeing my daughters, who also live in California, the impending trip worried me, since I'd not traveled alone for more than fifteen years and didn't know whether I could get from here to there with my impaired hearing—and mis-hearing—of public announcements. I was also troubled by the likelihood that this might be the last time I see my brother alive, or the last time he'd be present enough to converse and enjoy such an occasion, beset as he is by extreme heart failure. A hail-and-farewell I've been dreading the last few years.

Though our paths did not cross much during Marshall's worldwide research career, we bonded during childhood after the death of our parents, a loss that endowed us with an abiding concern for each other. Indeed, we've often been in touch by phone, not only keeping track of each other, but also urging each other away from risky activities. I can still hear the urgency in his voice, warning me against the dangers of smoking during my twenties and thirties, though I didn't quit until my late forties. And I remember urging him in his mid seventies not to fly too soon after his first stroke, but he didn't heed my warnings. We have both paid the price of our willfulness.

Beset by such thoughts, I drove to the airport wearing a black mesh running shoe on one foot and a brown leather walking shoe on the other. My toes had hurt so much from a pair of shoes I'd bought the day before that I tried on the others to see which would be more comfortable for the trip. Preoccupied after breakfast with getting to the airport in time for check-in, I didn't notice those mismatched shoes until I deboarded the plane in Minneapolis, looked down, and discovered the mix-up, then thought about aging and inattentiveness. I hurried to an airport men's store and bought a pair of light-brown, airy sheepskin walking shoes just right for summer. A happy conclusion to the screw-up, since the store also shipped home the others, free of charge.

Better still, the flight to Minneapolis was hassle-free, the in-flight announcements audible, and the mammoth airport easy to get around in, so it was a pleasure to be flying solo. Also pleasurable during a trouble-free flight to Sacramento. By the time I spied Amy waiting at the foot of the escalator to the baggage claim area, my pre-flight worry had given way to a heady sense of accomplishment, when all I'd done was to take a couple of comfortable flights. How strange to have been fretful after years of frequent air-travel during my academic career, as if age had left me a fearful child. Good reason to be elated at the first sight of Amy.

The headiness of it all continued on the way to Davis in Amy's new Honda, having her chauffeur me around when not so long ago, it seemed, I was driving her to Madison for her first year at Wisconsin. That memory reminded me of how the mind works, leaping from a ride of the moment to one that took place more than forty years ago, when Amy and I were much younger, talking of things like dorm arrangements. Which made me think it was almost ludicrous to have recalled that ride of long ago.

But the past asserts itself one way or another, as it did when we pulled up in front of Hannah's house, and she emerged with

Monty, both looking younger than I knew them to be, as if in their forties or fifties, though she's on the verge of sixty and he's sixty-five. Then I was struck by how different their house looked from the last time I'd been there—half the front now concealed by a large fig tree. Had all that growth taken place in just a few years, or had I forgotten how much time had passed since my last visit? Or do fig trees grow much faster than I imagined? Or has my advanced age made me unfit to judge the age of anything— people, houses, or trees? The interior is just as surprising, walls covered with artwork upstairs and down, much of it by Hannah, like a forty-year retrospective of her work, featuring an octet of her exquisite leaf prints. Nature into art her current project. The walls also hold some striking pieces inherited from Monty's parents, including a Grant Wood landscape of the undulant Iowa countryside that took me back home again.

I was surprised again when my son, Marshall, and my twenty-five-year-old grandson, Owen, showed up for dinner at Hannah and Monty's. No wonder my head was spinning, especially when I realized it was the first time in sixteen years I'd broken bread with all my children all at once and one of my grandchildren to boot. A family reunion before the morrow's larger reunion of my brother and his kids and some of their kids together with me and my kids and some of their kids—a gathering of Klauses the likes of which we've never had before. And probably will never have again, given the frailty of my brother.

But I didn't let that thought dilute the joy, except at noon the next day when my brother's stepson and caretaker, Geoff, lifted him and his oxygen tank out of a car into a wheelchair in front of his daughter Laura's house. A ceaseless traveler and lecturer, now unable to exit a car on his own or utter words that might do justice to the moment at hand. Then we were all in Laura's living room, beholding Marshall in his wheelchair, gracing us with a big smile as we sang "Happy birthday to you." Then like butterflies in a garden, we fluttered around each other, sipping the nectar of conversation, of catch-up, of reunion. Which made me wonder why we waited so long to have one, while many families get together every few years. Were we both too busy, Marshall and I, plowing our own fields? Or was it the lack of such a tradition among our forebears and thus the same for us and our children? Whatever the causes, all of us were buoyant at Marshall's ninetieth. The next day, we continued the celebration of his life and of the family, thanks to a bountiful luncheon and tributes arranged by his wife, Phyllis.

Amid all the festivities, I felt compelled to talk with Marshall alone, for Geoff had told me his severe heart failure meant "we could lose him any time now." I arranged to visit him the next morning at the retirement home where he lives with Phyllis and Geoff. I wanted to bid him farewell, but knowing his intense will to survive, an overt farewell was out of the question, especially during his birthday celebration. Better, I thought, to share recollections of our boyhood years in Cleveland and thus affirm our brotherly bond. Given the persistence of his long-term memory, evident in our phone conversations, I assumed he'd be up to such talk. And sure enough, when I reminded him of living with Uncle Manny, an M.D. like our father and a great humanitarian, Marshall was effusive, "Oh, he was very very special. Very special. He took such good care of us, of everyone." And he was effusive too when I mentioned Aunt Celia's German-Hungarian cooking, especially her incomparable slow-baked stew of spicey meatballs, beef brisket, and plump kosher franks, each of the meats separated from the others by layers of sauerkraut and canned tomatoes, yielding tangy and redolent juices ideal for serving over mashed potatoes. After savoring our memories of that remarkable dish, I reminded him that we only lived with Manny seven years before he died. Marshall readily picked up the thread and talked about Uncle Dan, our father's youngest brother, whom we lived with next in a narrow attic room. "What a difference with Dan. He was terrible, just terrible, wouldn't even get me a cab to the hospital when I got the polio."

Though up to the give and take, he occasionally nodded off

in the midst of talking to him, a sign of extreme heart failure I hadn't seen during Laura's party. Those nod-offs made me fear the imminence of his demise, but each lapse was brief, and then he was awake and talking about the origins of our forebears—the German-Hungarian heritage of our father's parents, the Lithuanian background of our mother's. So, I looked forward to another conversation the next morning. But Phyllis's birthday party for him that afternoon, with tributes from family, friends, and medical colleagues, left him so tired the next day it was all he could do to talk a bit about the party and "our wonderful visit" before nodding off at length. Which I took as a sign to give him a hug and my love and then to leave.

Walking down the empty hallway from his apartment to the elevator, I thought, "so this is how it ends, closing a door and walking away," the same thought that beset me when I walked out of the hospital room where Kate died. Such a bleak remembrance, I was grateful to see Hannah in the lobby, waiting to drive us back to Davis for yet another reunion I hadn't expected. This time not only with my children but also with their mother, my first wife, Meredith. Fifty-three years since the five of us had been together as a family. But when we sat down for dinner at Hannah and Monty's, the conversation felt almost as easy and comfortable as if we'd never been apart, except when I asked Meredith about her friends from college, and she told me of their demise. I was touched that she asked when I'd be coming again and hoped it wouldn't be too long. Then I gave her a big hug before Amy took her back home for the evening. In advanced age, every reunion, it seems, ends with ominous partings.

Back home the next evening, I was confident of seeing Meredith again, but didn't have such hopes for my brother, especially after getting word the next day of a fainting spell that led to hospitalization. Several days later he was released to hospice care in his retirement home, the doctors expecting he wouldn't last more than two or three weeks. But he hung on more than two months, until the morning of August 15. At the start of those final months, he told his daughter, Laura, "I'm gonna beat this, I'm gonna beat this." And two weeks later she sent an email reporting that "Dad has improved quite a lot. His swelling is way down. Today he was pretty clear when I was with him for a little while and shared my lunch and cherries."

But from then on, her reports noted a continuing decline, in which he slept or dozed more often than waking, spoke only from time to time and often didn't make sense, ate less and less, until he was quite thin, surviving on supplement drinks. A grim process, with several periods of agitation, one that climaxed in an outcry to talk with our mother, then our grandmother, then with me. At that moment in mid July, Phyllis called, put him on the phone, and he immediately asked, "How are you doing, how you doing," as he often had in the past. And as often before, I replied with an upbeat, "Well, and how about you?" To which he replied, as never before, "Not so well, not so well"—the last words of his I ever heard. A revelation that however out of it he might have been in the days and weeks before or after that call, he was aware of his dire situation. In the wake of that episode, he received morphine to help ease the agitation and pain, as well as Ativan to calm anxiety. But the episodes continued into early August.

Given Laura's continuing updates and my brother's extended agitation, I came to see that despite the thoughtful palliative care he received throughout his time in hospice, he was still extremely agitated at the prospect of dying. Which led me to revisit Atul Gawande's *Being Mortal: Medicine and What Matters in the End*, a detailed and compelling discussion of hospice, hoping it might ease my thoughts at the prospect of my brother's impending death. But when I reached Gawande's chapter on "Letting Go," I realized how difficult it would be for Marshall to do so after a lifetime of life-saving efforts on behalf of life-threatened newborns. If he could beat death for them, why not for himself, especially after a lifetime of beating the odds against his own longevity? His agitation at the imminence of death made me hope I'll "go gently into that good night."

Later in August, that thought came to mind again, when my son Marshall came for a long weekend to finish the basement clearout we worked on last year, and this year we finished the job. Shelves of plant pots, seeding trays, and canning jars from summers past boxed up and carted to charitable thrift shops. Surplus terrace blocks, gardening tools, and cooking equipment to local friends. Cartons of tree planting documents and local tree surveys from Kate's Heritage Trees Project to the City's forestry department. A remembrance of things past, especially when I gave Marshall a box of all the glass, wood, woven, straw, and glittery fish ornaments I collected for Christmas trees of yore. Emblems too of our fishing together in waters near and far. Letting go is a way of passing things on to others near and far.

Eighty-Five 🖋

A Superior Vacation, Octogenarian Exemplars

A year ago last September, when Jackie and I were vacationing on Lake Superior, we booked the most unusual cabin we'd ever seen. A timber-framed structure thirty feet from the lake, named Agate Beach Cabin, was the smallest place we ever rented. At just 325 square feet of living space—less than one-third the area of my home's first floor, yet it felt more spacious than the larger cabins we've stayed in, thanks to its peaked ceiling, open floor plan, and light-filled room. Cozy too, with its interior of knotty pine, beamed ceiling and angled supporting beams. It was equipped as well with a fine kitchen, bathroom, and laundry appliances.

The day before we drove there last fall, my nephrologist gave me a blunt reality check: "You're almost certain to need dialysis in the next two or three years." She made that assertion in response to one of mine, which I had thought would elicit approval: "Last month, I put myself on a kidney-preservation diet—low salt, low potassium, low phosphorus—to avoid dialysis." So, I was troubled by her definitive prediction, until my internist's blood check in early November revealed a slight improvement and elicited her opinion that "your kidneys are fairly stable." She was certainly more encouraging than my nephrologist about the diet and about the need for dialysis, albeit with a touch of gallows humor: "I don't think you're likely to need dialysis in the near future, if your kidney function remains as stable as it is right now, and you might never need it, given the possibility of some other condition doing you in before then." The wit of her final twist didn't surprise me, for a few minutes earlier, when she asked if I was still keeping this journal and I said, "Yes, but I've been feeling so good that my story might not speak to the medical problems of other eighty-year-olds," she said, "Don't worry about that; you've got more than enough on your chart to write about." So, my numerous health issues are a boon for writing, even as they're a risk to living.

They're also a spur to delightful getaways, like the two weeks we spent in our dream cabin back in September. Walking the nearby beach was a special pleasure. Though I didn't come upon any of the agates for which the cabin is named, I did find a piece of gray driftwood, its smooth surface polished by waves, and Jackie got a shot on her iPhone, showing the moon and its shaft of light illuminating the waves.

When we weren't enjoying the shore and the waves, we hiked a few trails far from the cabin and one morning beheld sweeping vistas of a forested mountainside. That afternoon, we drove along a narrow county road, eager to see where it would take us. A handmade sign beckoned toward a turnoff onto a one-lane gravel road with a string of little houses—an isolated settlement in the forest—that ended at a newly-sided house alongside an old trailer, a little shack, and an outhouse. As we pulled into the driveway, intending to back out and turn around, a man came out of the house with a welcoming wave, followed by a woman. He introduced himself as Bill, a retired Minnesota surveyor, and she as Jean, a retired nurse who used to work at the Mayo Clinic. After we told them about ourselves and our whereabouts, Bill invited us to see their place, and he showed us not only the unfinished house they're working on, but also the compact trailer that's been their vacation home in years past, the shack that contains both a sauna and their compact sleeping spot, as well as the outhouse with two stools. Then he led us to an idyllic lake with game fish, just a few steps from their backyard.

Though neither Bill nor Jean is physically imposing, both are quite vigorous compared to Jackie and me, so they didn't seem old enough to be retired. I wondered out loud if the new house would become their new vacation home, but Jean set me straight—"It'll be our new home year-round. We're coming up here to live permanently." A daring venture, so far away from it all, it made our brief September getaway in a luxurious cabin seem like a frivolous version of their true grit lifestyle, especially given the severe challenges of northern Minnesota winters. Driving back to our cabin, I felt at once humbled by the encounter and grateful to have met those self-reliant people. From then on, I also felt a bit sheepish about lunching at our favorite spots in Grand Marais, rather than cooking at our cabin, but the grilled mackerel at the Angry Trout always got the better of me.

Back home in mid September, I took part in a photo shoot, posing beside my house for a full-page ad in *Preservation Magazine*. Published by the National Trust for Historic Preservation, the ad encourages readers to donate their home, as I did several years ago. Mark, the photographer, posed me in three different settings—on a loveseat in the living room, on a porch swing, and standing on the front lawn with a full view of the house directly behind me. In all of his shots at various angles and distances, the house looks splendid. But despite his suggestions to relax and smile, I couldn't do much better than a stiff, artificial grin. Nothing like a full Duchenne smile. A few months later, it was a pleasure to see that in the published shot, I'm standing off to the side, while the old brick house and its gabled roof dominate the image.

I'd much rather behold others or the work of others, as I did in the process of a brief course that Jackie and I attended on the subject of National Parks and how they have inspired American landscape art. The series of four weekly two-hour lectures during October was meticulously prepared and delivered by Joni, a

University of Iowa professor of art history. Thanks to her extensive slide collection, we saw vivid images week in and week out that made me wish the course had continued the entire fall, especially given Joni's deft weave of history, biography, analysis, and appreciation.

Aside from Joni's lectures, my early fall days were devoted to the flower and vegetable gardens, the unpredictable stock market, and the question of how to celebrate my brother's life at his upcoming memorial in November. Putting the gardens to bed was the easy part, thanks to Isabella, thorough and speedy as ever. But the high-priced stock market troubled me again in mid October, so I sold all the stock in both my IRA and personal account. Had I been fifteen or twenty years younger, with time to recover from a drastic market collapse, I might have sold only a third or half of my holdings. But at eighty-five, the hope of recouping one's losses is a pipe dream. Now, I have fifty percent of that cash in risk-free three-year CDs, yielding 2.5 percent at my local credit union, and half of the remainder in Vanguard's short-term corporate bond ETF, yielding about 2.2 percent, and the rest in cash, waiting for a substantial correction before reinvesting anything in stocks. Since then, the market has increased so much more, I'm sometimes dismayed by the lost profits and the looming tax bill on capital gains, until I remember that my father, a multimillionaire doctor, lost everything he owned in the crash of 1929.

While reducing my investment risks, I pondered a tribute to my brother's remarkable life not only in the wake of our parents' deaths, but also in the aftermath of the polio that beset him during his third year of medical school. Though the fact of such losses is well known in and out of the family, no one but me had firsthand recollections of him from childhood to his time in medical school. Though it seemed imperative to share those memories, I didn't know how to introduce them until I received a tribute from our ninety-one-year-old cousin David, who was unable to attend, so asked me to read it at the service. David's tribute began with a story I'd never heard before—of my brother punching him in the face when they were young children, a punch that gave me the metaphor I needed to celebrate my brother's lifetime of perseverance—always putting up a good fight.

The memorial weekend was more comforting than I expected, not only because of Jackie's companionship, but also because of compelling tributes by his children and colleagues, as well as the scattering of his ashes at a panoramic site overlooking the Santa Cruz mountains. A mild, sunny day put us in a fitting mood for the gentle hike to the spot Laura had chosen for the occasion. Since no one else had ever taken part in such an affair, and some were uneasy even about touching his ashes, Laura and Phyllis asked me to head up the ceremony, given my prior experience of scattering Kate's ashes on the north shore of Kauai. I began by reciting an Emily Dickinson poem, befitting the occasion and the lovely fall day of our gathering— "These are the days when birds come back"—scattering some of his ashes as I did so, in hope of stimulating others to do so. By the time I reached the concluding lines, others had come forward to scatter his ashes, with such visible expressions of comfort that it was gratifying to behold the communal bonding.

A few weeks later, Jackie and I enjoyed a festive occasion with a wry reminder of mortality at the eightieth birthday party for our friend Zoe, a gentle and generous person, a faint smile always gracing her face. Hosted by her children, their spouses, and her grandchildren, the party was a rainbow of young and old, notable and otherwise, jammed into her nineteenth-century home, enjoying champagne and wine, as well as a lavish spread of delicacies, featuring asparagus wrapped in prosciutto, smoked salmon mousse, and petit fours galore. A scrumptious array climaxed by a three-tiered birthday cake, surrounded by diminutive wooden figures, one for each of her children and grandchildren. A confection nonpareil produced by her daughter Leah, food writer for the *Chicago Tribune*, featured a two-layered almond cake, the layers separated by thin bands of apricot surrounding a thin band of meringue. It was covered with a chocolate buttercream frosting infused with rum. The whole of it could be described only by the word that sprang from my mouth after the first bite—"erotic," which provoked nodding heads all around. But my description of the cake could hardly compare to Zoe's description of the bash—"It's a memorial." Which explains why she was dressed in a floor-length black outfit and had a photomontage of her life playing on TV in the front room. "All the better," I said, "because you're here to enjoy it." An octogenarian fantasy.

Enjoyment was the last thing we expected a few days later, on the way to visit our friend Hank—eighty-eight and bedridden in the hospital after a bizarre set of maladies that began with acute pain in a hip that had been replaced a year or so ago. Imaging tests indicated no problem in the hip, but did reveal an abdominal aneurysm. Surgical repair was delayed because of Hank's age and the onset of a tenacious lung infection that weakened him so much he was put on oxygen. Though he was emaciated, his eyes barely open and voice very soft, he was still his feisty self—sitting straight up in bed, head erect, cracking jokes, verbally sparring with his devoted son Mark, grumbling about the hospital food. He kept nodding off, given the difficulty of breathing, even on oxygen. Yet it was heartening to see that this former CEO, emeritus professor, and co-op treasurer was still as determined as when he was playing tennis a few years ago after a knee replacement surgery, and replied to my chiding concern with a quick comeback—"if you don't push your body and push it hard, you'll lose it. It's as simple as that." On the other hand, there's a time when one's body refuses to be pushed any longer, as with Hank a week after our visit.

In hope of postponing that refusal, I attended a two-hour program on dialysis in early December, as recommended by my nephrologist. The session provided information about the technicalities and challenges of dialysis, which made me even more fiercely committed to the diet I've been using since mid August. The dietitian's presentation revealed that I have to be even more stringent than before, limiting dairy products as much as possible in order to reduce phosphorus intake to levels that can be processed by compromised kidneys. Since then, I've abandoned milk altogether for the first time in my life, and now enjoy my breakfast strawberries, blueberries, and red raspberries with cranberry juice, or without any liquid at all. And I've given up other dairy products. Goodbye butter, cream, yogurt, and ice cream. To keep potassium intake to manageable levels, I've also abandoned a host of other favorites, such as avocados, bananas, potatoes, and chocolate. A goodbye to many scrumptious things, but then I remembered all the wonderful fruits, vegetables, meats, rices, and pastas I can still enjoy. Aging, after all, continues to require a series of trade-offs.

A few days after the dialysis talks, Jackie and I attended a more enjoyable presentation at a local staging of *Joseph and the Amazing Technicolor Dreamcoat* that featured a gifted high school senior as Joseph's brother Benjamin, doing such an agile, free-form, and energetic calypso dance that he seemed destined for Broadway. In the midst of that solo, his joyous expression, his exceptional gestures and movements seemed irrepressible, unstoppable— emblems of what it takes to steal a show, upstaging everyone around him, including Joseph. What I didn't fully realize until the show was over, as we walked by the lad in the lobby and saw him behaving no differently from everyone around, is how utterly transforming it must be to perform on stage in the glitter of lights for the pleasure of a large audience.

The early days of January also brought a brief but memorable visit from Jackie's daughter Mindy and her wife Mary, who divide their time between Georgetown and New Orleans. They are both such accomplished historians and political observers that being with them is always stimulating. Especially when Mary, a notable octogenarian, formerly chair of the U.S. Civil Rights Commission, holds forth—this time, not surprisingly, on Trump. "He didn't expect to win the presidency, he didn't even want the presidency, so it's not surprising that neither he nor his advisors were ready for it." Mary, it seems, is so often on her soapbox, especially in TV commentaries, that Mindy was delighted to find an antique wooden soapbox here in town and to give her. Soapboxes are relics of how public speakers in years past elevated themselves, the better to be seen and heard, though I didn't know of that use when I took part in a soapbox derby during my childhood days in Cleveland.

The last night of their visit, I got another taste of Mary's way with words, as well as her competitive savvy, in a game of Scrabble that Jackie and Mindy arranged in order to pit Mary and me against each other. Memorable because I scored more than Mary until the last play of the game, when she won by using up her last five letters in a single move that reversed the score and ended the game. The surprising turn of events left me wondering whether she made a lucky draw of letters at the end, or had held back several in hope of making such a coup de grace. Whatever the case, my luck had run out.

That game and that thought came to mind a week or so later when I read an interview with Phillip Roth, another notable octogenarian, in the *New York Times*, responding to the question of what growing old has been like: "It's something like playing a game, day in and day out, a high-stakes game that for now, even against the odds, I just keep winning. We will see how long my luck holds out."

Eighty-Five to Eighty-Six ✒
Ups, Downs, Yoga, Heeding a Heat Wave

FEBRUARY 2018 TO AUGUST 2018

The past six months began on a high note, with a reading from this work to an enthusiastic crowd at the local senior center, which made me feel like a notable author, thanks to a big turnout on a bitterly cold afternoon in early February. From congratulatory emails and phone calls to requests for additional readings, I was on cloud nine, which led me to write a euphoric Valentine poem to Jackie:

VALENTINE 2018

Oh Valentine, dear Valentine,
We're oh so far from thirty-nine,
And forty-nine and fifty-nine,
We're closer now to eighty-nine.
How long we've aged upon the vine,
Like grapes that make the grandest wine!
So I'll be yours if you'll be mine,
To make a vintage extra fine.

Two days later, I was still in the clouds when Jackie and I visited Dick and Phyllis again in Rancho Mirage—its summery California air a blessing after the deep-freeze of Iowa. Their yard is a technicolor mirage—bright green lawn, beige palm trees, pendulous lemon trees, turquoise pool, and white lounge chairs, creating a vivid backdrop for its vigorous inhabitants, both eighty-four and undaunted by their infirmities. Though Dick's knees are painful, he's as active and upbeat as when we visited last year. Though Phyllis is still recovering from hip replacement, she not only works out with her trainer three days a week but also prepares delicious meals every day.

During our visit, Dick drove us to visit Bill, another indomitable friend from Iowa City, who bought a small concrete-block house a few years ago on the outskirts of Joshua Tree National Park and has spent a month or so each year deconstructing its interior in order to construct within its 880 square feet a Bauhaus-style residence in the midst of the desert. All the remodeling—beamed ceiling, white walls, and flooring—done by Bill himself. An admirable eighty-one-year-old, aging without compromise despite a heart attack several months ago.

Flying back to Iowa the next day, I didn't expect anything to go amiss, especially not in front of my house at 12:30 in the morning, until the airport shuttle turned into the driveway and slipped back into the street—again and again. Though the driver offered to carry my luggage up to the house, I declined, given his cab full of passengers, including Jackie. As he drove away, I discovered an incline so icy that a step or two up was followed by a slide back, again and again. There was no way to get to the house but to get on my hands and knees and crawl up the 125-foot driveway, dragging my luggage behind me. The crawling was slow and arduous, given the dense snow, my wonky heart, and the below-freezing cold, which led me to stop and rest again and again until reaching the top, twenty minutes later. Knees soaked, hands chilled, body shaking, especially after pulling the luggage and myself up to a standing position. Next time, I'll know better than to refuse someone's help in a situation like that.

A few weeks after that painful experience, I had a painless one at the office of my dentist, who drilled out a filling with decay behind it, cleaned out the infection, and refilled it—without a pain-killing injection to begin with, yet I felt no pain, even when he shoved a metal clamp into my gum to guide the gold filling. I couldn't understand the lack of pain, until he explained that "with aging, the nerves in your teeth become small, so you're less able to feel pain from tooth decay or gum disease." An upside of aging, I thought, until I consulted a few internet sites on aging and tooth pain, which all noted that the lack of pain caused by aging can result in irreparable decay. The loss of sensation in my teeth is akin to the loss of it in the tips of my fingers, so that I can't button my shirts without a visual search for the buttonholes.

The aging brain also declines as its synapses fail, but the consequences of its decline are sometimes so conspicuous they're difficult to ignore, as Jackie reminded me in early March when I told her about *45 Years*, a compelling movie on TV the night before. Starring two of my favorite British actors, Tom Courtenay and Charlotte Rampling, it dramatizes the disintegration of a seemingly happy marriage during the week leading up to the couple's forty-fifth anniversary. When I started to tell Jackie about it, she not only remembered some of the important details but also told me we had watched it together on a disc she rented a while back. Yet I watched the movie again as if I'd never seen it before—stark evidence of severe forgetfulness, especially of movies I've seen and books I've read the past few years, when my brain has evidently not been storing things as well as before. I wonder how to remedy the problem, and the only answer that comes to mind is the one I've been using for this chronicle—making notes on the most compelling movies I see and the most compelling books I read. Writing, after all, is an aid to memory and a distillation of experience.

Forgetfulness rarely beset me when I was still in the classroom, still involved in the rapid give-and-take of discussion. But when I mentioned that memory to my poet friend Marvin at a going-away party for a fellow author, he was quick with a comeback—"It's the new normal, man. Get used to it. You're now a geezer. And being in the classroom wouldn't be of any help." An assertion confirmed a while later, when I was repeatedly at a loss for words and thoughts.

Two days after the forgotten-movie episode, I forgot to take my morning blood pressure meds—the first time in forty-eight years—and didn't discover the lapse until it was time to take my evening meds some twelve hours later and found the untaken pills in my pajama pocket. A lapse that led to highly elevated blood pressure, so Jackie drove me to the emergency room the next morning, where the doctor diagnosed an episode of atrial fibrillation—the first recurrence since the debilitating one more than two years ago. Intravenous drugs the next few hours lowered the blood pressure enough that when I asked the attending physician if Jackie and I could keep a dinner engagement with friends, he approved with a playful smile, "assuming you want to have dinner with them." Speedy as it was at the emergency room, the aftermath involved several days of medical consultation, medication changes, pre-bedtime calming measures to deal with insomnia, and a month of twice-daily blood pressure checks at home to monitor the effectiveness of the new medication. All of which has made me more vigilant than before.

After that scary episode and my memory of the mental lapse that caused it, I was delighted by the story of a life much different from my own, when Jackie and I watched *Jane*, the National Geographic documentary about Jane Goodall, now eighty-four. Having yearned to live in Africa and "come as close to talking to animals as possible," she moved there from London in 1956, and in 1960 to the Gombe forest, where she spent more than fifty-five years observing and detailing the behavior of chimpanzees. Her lifelong project was "to show how like us they are"—in their tool use, their affectionate hugging and grooming, and their territorial aggression. Given her dedication to that project, Goodall sacrificed her marriage rather than abandon her study of chimpanzees.

Shortly after watching Goodall and the chimps, Jackie and I were impressed by the story of a very different person in Ina

Loewenberg's *A Life à la Carte*. A local personage, eighty-six years old, she has graduate degrees not only in philosophy but also in accounting; she has worked in tax preparation as well as hospital auditing; and since 1986, she has been devoted to the art of photography. In addition to being a devoted wife and mother, she has edited *The View from 70: Women's Recollections and Reflections*, a unique work in which she and forty-one others, all born in 1931, share their perceptions of the world as young women and at seventy, with photographs of them as young women and as seventy-year-olds.

The lives of Goodall and Loewenberg differ in so many ways that, except for being in their mid eighties, it might seem as if they have nothing in common, especially given their recent activities—Goodall traveling most of the year in support of chimpanzees and the environment, Loewenberg leading a poetry reading group at the local senior center. Despite those striking differences, they're both devoted to the well-being of the world, and both doing so as long as they can. Aging as purposefully as possible.

After learning about Goodall and Loewenberg, I was puzzled at the start of the movie *Lucky*, wondering why Harry Dean Stanton, a masterful and versatile actor, spent the last few months of his life playing the title role of a slacker. A gaunt ninety-year-old character dedicated to his trivial routines—his morning yoga, his glass of milk, his smoking, his TV programs, his crossword puzzle, his walk into town and back from a little home in the desert, and his brief encounters with nearby residents at the local coffee shop and bar—he seemed at first bereft of any serious commitment, except during an encounter with a former marine in the coffee shop, where he warms to a conversation about their time in the Philippines during World War II. Then, in the wake of a fall and a visit with the town doctor, it becomes clear that there's more to Lucky than his daily routines, when his intense consciousness of mortality is revealed and later, in the bar, his combative atheism. Another side of Lucky is reflected in the mournful rendition of "Red River Valley" that he often plays on a harmonica and that echoes in the background music—an expression of lost love and painful yearning so intense it wells up in his spontaneous singing of "Volver, Volver" at the birthday fiesta for a young boy.

But why have I dwelt on such a late life story as Lucky's and Stanton's? Partly because they suggest that purposefulness exists even where one might least expect it, even in a slacker like Lucky. Partly because I recently received a message from my internist, who sent me a blank health care directive, asking for the appointment of a health care agent and for my preferences concerning CPR and life-prolonging treatments. Had I received that form several years ago before my recent medical problems, I would probably have considered it a routine informational request. But it now seems like an ominous sign that she sees a more calamitous event in the offing.

To distract myself from such fretting, in early April I ventured into the world of yoga via "Yoga with a Chair"—the less demanding form of it for aged folks like me and the nine women enrolled in our weekly, two-month-long class. But even with the aid of a chair and the gentle attentiveness of our instructor, Robin, I was at a loss, given my ignorance of yoga, my bent-over posture, my mouth-breathing habit, and my overeagerness to perform the unfamiliar poses as well as possible, without knowing a thing about how to coordinate inhales and exhales with the movements in each pose. I felt at first like a fish out of water, flapping my gills and body on dry land, especially trying to do the warrior poses and single-leg balances at the same time as elevated arm movements.

During the next few weeks, I practiced the basic body movements and coordinated breathing patterns at home. But balancing on one foot while holding my hands up in a prayer pose continued to bedevil me. So I told Robin about my problems, and she told me of the need for patience—"your vegetables take time to grow and mature, and the same is true with yoga exercises and poses." Thoughtful advice that led me to enroll in the next eight-week session, feeling more relaxed than before.

Jackie, by contrast, was beset in late April with such severe pain in her right thigh, leg, and foot that she consulted a physical therapist, who diagnosed the problem as sciatica, caused by a pinched nerve in the lower back. He recommended some challenging exercises that Jackie performed twice a day, but the pain recurred after sitting too long and on other occasions. Jackie has rarely spoken about pain in our fifteen years together; this time she was quite fatigued for a while, especially since it took almost two months of therapy and exercises to remedy the problem. Meanwhile, Jackie continued her twice-weekly workouts without missing a beat, as if she could work her way out of the pain.

She also laughed her way out of pain when Ed Asner, now eighty-eight, came to town in the title role of *A Man and His Prostate*, an uproarious monologue full of off-color jokes and verbal byplay by a character with prostate troubles that beset him in the midst of a vacation in Italy. Though it focuses on the prostate, his monologue bears witness to the debilities of old age, for it frequently alludes to his infirmities, evident in Asner's lined face and stiff movements on stage. And the play's deliberately aroused laughter—all of us in the theater laughing like Jackie—embodies an approach to aging made explicit in his parting commitment "to live as if we're never going to die."

I wish it were possible to do so as in years past, but having recently turned eighty-five, I'm troubled by a remark that Phillip Roth made after he turned eighty-five—that despite "the illusion this thing is never going to end . . . it can stop on a dime." And it did for Roth four months after he made that assertion. So, the news of his death was not entirely surprising, though it was certainly haunting, given that I'm a year older than he and afflicted with the same heart problems. No wonder a woman at my Oaknoll reading in May was worried that "some of us might not be here to read your book if it doesn't come out until 2021."

Shortly after the reading at Oaknoll, I decided to turn my large all-season garden plot back into grass. Once a cornucopia of vegetables and the inspiration for *My Vegetable Love*, it's now partly shaded by a pin oak that Kate and I planted forty-seven years ago. Given how few vegetables I've grown there the past several years—and how little energy or will I've had for tending such a large plot—I should have accepted the inevitability of closing it down last year or the year before. Letting go, letting go. But I'm still able to tend the small summer plot of tomatoes, eggplants, and peppers, the sight of which makes me eager for August, when they're ripe enough for a Mediterranean stew with basil and oregano from the herb bed. But before then it's also a pleasure to watch the tomato plants setting fruit and climbing up the seven-foot supporting stakes after having started them from seed in early March. Though I know they'll be undone by the first hard frost in October, the busyness of digging deep and transplanting them deep in late May is an exhilarating moment in late spring.

Jackie and I celebrated the first day of June by driving to Des Moines with Stan and Pat to behold an array of creatures in spacious settings at the Blank Park Zoo. The only accredited zoo in Iowa, it was launched by Jackie and her former husband Alan in 1963, and since then has grown into a twenty-five-acre park with hundreds of familiar and exotic species—from alligators, bonobos, and cave bats to snow leopards, wallabies, and zebu. A rare pleasure to behold them, but by late morning the heat was so intense and burdensome the animals were not moving, and one of the giant tortoises was hidden within its shell, which made me wish that I too could hide so effectively from the heat. Though we left at noon and got back in midafternoon after an air-conditioned ride, I was exhausted by the heat, went to bed at nine and slept until seven the next morning.

That experience and newspaper articles about aged people undone by high temperatures should have made me very cautious when the next heat wave arrived, especially given my longtime heart problems. But I was slow on the uptake, even after vowing to stay in air-conditioned settings when the outdoor temperature is above eighty-five. Early on in the heat wave, I agreed to a late afternoon outing with friends of Jackie, and despite sitting at a shaded table with a pleasant breeze, several hours later the heat had driven my blood pressure up to 172/97. Since then, I've not broken the vow and neither has Jackie, after a few dizzy spells of her own.

Thanks to the exceptional heat wave in early June, I spent a few days inside cleaning the house in advance of an inspection by Jan, an architectural historian, who prepared an excellent report of it for nomination to the National Register of Historic Places. During another heat wave in late June, I spent several days not only reading the *Iowa Driver's Manual*, relearning the rules of the road and all the signs that make them explicit, but also taking sample tests of my knowledge in preparation for the possibility that I might have to take a driving test to get my license renewed.

Despite the reassurances of my lawyer friend Nancy, I was panicked at the thought of failing it and having to give up my car and the mobility that enables me to live on my own in this house. A fear that bedevils many aged people. After study sessions inside, I spent three days outside practicing the basics of driving with both hands on the wheel in the ten-o'clock/two-o'clock position and driving and turning in accordance with regulations that determine the right-of way in a wide range of situations, as well as practicing how to parallel park and how to execute a three-point U-turn.

After a week of study and practice and an excellent vision report from my optometrist, I felt well prepared, but still nervous about the possibility of a driving test. The nervousness didn't end until the examiner gave me an unexpected test, an oral exam, asking me to tell him the time of day, the day of the week, the month, the year, the city, the state, my birthday, my height, and my home address, all of which I answered correctly, followed by his directive to face the camera and smile. And I did.

Mid July brought admirable news from my friend and former colleague Gene, now eighty-five, whom I hadn't seen since he stayed with Kate and me in 2002, the weekend she died. Though he's emailed me from time to time, I had no idea he's been writing all these years, thanks to my having forgotten two remarkable works of fiction he published and sent me during those years. They only came to mind after reading his email, which included an announcement of his new novel, *The House of Nordquist*, the last of three experimental works in The Eroica Trilogy, a heroic achievement that made me hope his venturesome works might be made into films.

Closer to home, the last week in July brought an unusual encounter with a gray-haired stranger eyeballing my twenty-two-year-old car when I walked out of the co-op—"Do you wanna sell that Jeep?" Though touched by his interest, I quickly declined: "I couldn't afford a new car and couldn't part with this old friend." Walking away, he smiled and said, "It's perfect for geezers like us." As proof of my geezerdom, the next day at a gas station, I tried to fill my tank with diesel fuel, but the nozzle wouldn't fit into the receptacle, though I tried several times without realizing the error, until a young woman filling her tank came over and set me straight. Which made me wonder how I'd have done on a driving test if I couldn't figure out how to fill my gas tank.

A couple of weeks later when Jackie and I went out for dinner with our friends Phil and Karen, I had a more comforting explanation of my geezerish foibles. While waiting for our meals to arrive, I was going on about my memory problems, after which Phil told me his idea that people in their eighties have lived so long and experienced so much that they cannot make room for new memories without sloughing off old ones. An appealing commonsensical idea, especially coming from a former philosophy professor, thoughtfully suggesting that the loss of old memories is offset by the gain of new ones. Such a tidy trade-off, however, that I couldn't help wondering whether it squares with current research. He told me of a piece in *Science* (May 8, 2014), reporting that "the first study of its kind in mice suggests that the brain may clear away old information in the process of forming new memories." My best new memories of the moment are that the heat wave has given way to mild temperatures and the tomatoes have now reached the top of their seven-foot supporting poles. No wonder I'm still smiling.

Eighty-Six ↙

Falling and Falling, Pain and Distractions, Body and Mind

AUGUST 2018 TO FEBRUARY 2019

In mid August, I was in the midst of Barbara Ehrenreich's *Natural Causes: An Epidemic of Wellness, the Certainty of Dying, and Killing Ourselves to Live Longer*. Its concern with aging, mortality, and longevity compelled my attention. But its grim view of aging—"above all an accumulation of disabilities"—doesn't square with my experience of it. Though I have numerous "health issues" on my medical chart, some quite serious, they are not disabling and not the overriding factor in my experience of aging. Indeed, I'm still able to traverse all the stairs in my four-story house; do my own shopping, cooking, and light housecleaning; exercise on the treadmill; and keep in touch with life in the backyard—feeding the birds, noting when the daffodils break ground, shooing away the deer, and raking the fall leaves.

A Pollyanna-like view, I admit, but just to make clear that the past six months have not been all rosy, in early September I fell headlong on the floor during a yoga class while doing a one-leg balance. Standing one second, falling the next, my arm extended in panic. A fall three days after a tornado felled my sixty-year-old black maple—its head, trunk, and branches spread across the back terrace and the surrounding lawn. No wonder I experienced a fear of falling in the days and weeks that followed. After the yoga fall, I felt so little pain that a few minutes later I stood up with a hand from Robin, and took part in the last thirty minutes of her class. Mindless behavior of a person in shock? Or a macho male display? Whatever the case, a week later when I began to feel unsteady on my feet and my right shoulder began to feel quite painful from breaking the fall with my right arm, I bid farewell to Robin and yoga, grateful that the outstretched arm had prevented my head from taking the brunt of it.

The fallen maple was a different story, a dinnertime nightmare. When Jackie and I first saw its massive head motionless on the terrace, minutes after a siren wailed and thunder cracked around the house, I was stunned into silence, calm as if nothing at all had happened, while she was in tears. My silence reminded me of how Kate's death had also left me absurdly calm, as if being so could quell the anguish. Calmly, then, I called my tree-man, Sebastian, told him of its demise, and asked him to take care of its remains. Then I pondered the huge hole in our life from the loss of that long-standing friend—no longer shading the house and terrace from the intense afternoon sun, no longer capable of its fiery fall display.

The brief tornado that did it in was so violent, I sought distraction in the memory of an antithetical dinnertime experience two weeks earlier, when Jackie and I had enjoyed a windless time on a nearby lake, thanks to our friend Sharon, who drove us to her pontoon boat with fixings for a tasty picnic supper. We boarded at 6:30 and didn't leave the water until 9:00, shortly after seeing the new moon with the old moon in its arms, an emblem of gentleness in a peaceful sky. Sharon was a water-wise counterpart, steering the boat from one leg of the lake to another without losing track of her thoughts, the boat, the shore, or us. A dream-like evening on the water, which transported me back some fifty years, fishing there with colleagues past and teaching my son how to wet a line in quiet coves around the lake. The memories put me in mind of "Once More to the Lake" and E. B. White's consciousness of how a long-cherished lake can seem timeless until one notices all the changes that have taken place around it, but I didn't let those changes intrude too long on the enduring image of the new moon with the old one in its arms.

Three weeks later, when Jackie and I would ordinarily have been in a cabin on Lake Superior, we traveled to a far different place in northern California for the wedding of my granddaughter Lizzie. She is a nursery school teacher and nanny, her husband, Tanner, a devoted angler and professional gardener. The site of their wedding was a grassy hillock surrounded by beige and green hills rolling into the distance of a 500-acre vineyard, which looked like the embodiment of an expansive future—a future envisioned in eloquent reflections on the challenges, obligations, and rewards of marriage by Lizzie's Aunt Kay.

I wish we had witnessed the event firsthand, but temperatures in the nineties were too risky for us octogenarians, so we huddled in a barn below while the ceremony we'd flown out to see took place on the hillock above us. A strange disconnect. We were there and not there, but grateful to Hannah and Monty for urging us to stay indoors. Several days later, we watched the ceremony on a video produced by Monty. Before and after the wedding, we dined not only with my children, grandchildren, and nieces, but also with Monty's brother, sister, and their spouses—not only with my former wife Meredith, but also with her sisters and brother, whom I'd not seen since she and I were divorced more than fifty years ago. All of us together again throughout the weekend, reminding me that weddings and reunions are akin—in a communion of families, in a marriage of present and past.

Returning home, I had a different kind of reunion, with the eight-foot maple tree trunk still rooted in the ground. A longer section of it was still on the terrace where it fell, inches from the house. Reminders of the tree's demise three weeks before. Given all the other downed trees to deal with, my arborist didn't have time to remove and grind the rooted trunk until several more weeks had passed. Meanwhile, the long flight home in a small airline seat had put so much pressure on Jackie's lower spine that it re-aggravated her sciatica and reignited intense pain throughout her right leg and thigh. It also left me with a swollen left leg and ankle, since I didn't have the good sense to walk the aisle several times during the flight. Our mutual leg problems led to mutual consolation, but Jackie had a much more hobbling and painful condition than I, and her sciatica was much less responsive to treatment than the edema in my leg. A few days on the treadmill helped to reduce the swelling, as did compression stockings recommended by my internist. So, a week after returning from California, I was in good enough shape to give another reading from this chronicle. But Jackie's leg exercises were very difficult and painful. And the sciatica continued to beset her throughout the fall and early winter, the pain sometimes so fierce it moved her to tears. After a month of it, she said "I'm not accustomed to such pain." And later put it another way: "For the first time in my life I'm feeling old, very old."

I once thought sciatica an affliction of the aged, but now realize that people in their forties and fifties also suffer from it, for it can be caused by any problem in the lower back that presses on the sciatic nerve, such as a damaged spine, compressed disks, or an enlarged cyst, as in Jackie's case. But the risk of neural damage from attempting to drain the cyst left few remedies for the pain, other than leg exercises, acupuncture, Tylenol (for brief periods of relief), or Gabapentin (for longer relief but with sleepy side effects). And none of those was helpful enough to relieve Jackie's increasing fatigue from pain-interrupted sleep, often reported in my notes of the past several months. The sciatica left her so exhausted and in pain that she sometimes canceled get-togethers with friends—exceptional behavior for someone as sociable and uncomplaining as she. After four months of sciatica, Jackie called it the new normal, but then in early January, announced that the pain had abated as surprisingly and inexplicably as it had done a few brief times during the fall. Now in late January as I'm writing this paragraph, it's still not troubling her, but she's aware it can afflict her again, given the prior interim of three or four painless months before it returned in early September.

While Jackie was suffering, I had a few problems of my own. A painful right shoulder kept me from sleeping on my favored right side, which caused a bout of interrupted sleep on the left side that wakened me four to six times a night. And I worsened it by checking the time at each wakening. But Tylenol, the passing of time, and resistance-band exercises gradually relieved the shoulder pain, which in turn relieved the interrupted sleep problem. My troubles, after all, were nothing compared to hers—a rare deviation from her uncommonly good health and my numerous health issues.

In the midst of our aches and pains, Jackie and I had an unusual experience at a local movie house, where we watched *Varieté*, a German silent movie, with live accompaniment by a local orchestra. A confessional tale of a callous, adulterous trapeze artist, driven to murder by one of his own kind, its grimness was underscored by the orchestra's haunting melodies. From start to finish, the movie and music were so absorbing that I forgot my pain. And Jackie forgot hers. Our identical reactions despite our physical and temperamental differences, as well as the different causes of our pain, made me realize that the experience of pain evidently depends not only on physical sensations but also on mental focus and awareness. A couple of hours later with nothing to distract me from the pain, I couldn't get to sleep for a couple of hours. Earlier that day, Jackie had been in so much pain that she asked me "will crying relieve the pain?" and then started crying as I held her and tried to comfort her. Several minutes later she said "that was a serious question," but I didn't know enough about crying or pain or the workings of our minds to venture an answer. On the other hand, we confirmed the power of good movies to distract us from the sensation of pain via films as different as *First Reformed*, the harrowing portrait of a deeply devoted but deeply troubled minister, and *Roma*, the coming-of-age story of a young boy in Mexico City under the care of a maid whose devotion to him and his family is vividly portrayed.

A senior college course on cognitive aging not only distracted us from our pain but also helped us to understand the workings of our aged minds. The instructor, a geropsychiatric nurse, began by outlining a cognitive spectrum from normal mental aging to mild cognitive impairment to the dementias—distinctions that proved instructive in assessing our own abilities (and prospects). According to that spectrum, it's clear that Jackie's exceptional memory and executive function reflect a very healthy aging brain, despite the occasional loss of a word or name that she frets about without any cause for worry. It's equally clear that my memory lapses combined with imperfect hearing and slow recall of recent experience are indicative of mild cognitive impairment—but not yet anything worse, given my ability to perform the basic activities of daily living, as well as to process, plan, and act on incoming information, as in this ongoing chronicle, and in deciding early this fall that my advanced age made it advisable to move all my IRA stock investments into risk-free CDs. I wish my cognitive impairment were equally risk-free.

But increasing age brings increasing risk of dementia (twenty-five percent of eighty-year-olds, thirty-three percent of eighty-five-year-olds, and fifty percent of ninety-year-olds), so I heed the research-based guidelines our instructor outlined for maintaining cognitive ability. A healthy Mediterranean diet, regular treadmill exercise, weight control, timely medical care, stimulating mental and social activities, seven to eight hours of sleep, stress management techniques, and a positive outlook on aging, unlike Ehrenreich's grim view of it. Better to live joyously, like Ed in *A Man and His Prostate*, despite the debilities of advanced age. In other words, an awareness that body and mind are interdependent, while also recognizing the importance of using systematic methods to think clearly, remember accurately, and make thoughtful decisions.

Thanks to the influence of those guidelines and a couple of

hernia flareups, I put myself on a carb-avoidance diet in hope of losing weight—no more corn chips, white rice, pastries, and the like. A decision that led me to make myself a salad like the scrumptious ones I've had every year when Jackie and I get lunch at the Angry Trout in Grand Marais: A bed of lettuce generously topped with a variety of fresh vegetables—cherry tomatoes, mounds of slivered beets and slivered carrots, as well as scatterings of sliced cucumbers, red onions, and radishes. I dressed this bountiful and colorful garden salad with a white wine vinaigrette and sided it with a grilled fillet of lake trout, as they do at the Angry Trout. A vivid stand-in for the ones I missed this September, when Jackie and I were in California rather than Grand Marais. Thanks to dietary restrictions, I lost fifteen pounds the last two months, put an end to the hernia flareups, and feel much better than before. Equally important with weight loss, I asked my internist to approve a moderate trial increase in one of my medications, with follow-up checks of blood pressure and side effects, which in combination with the weight-loss regimen produced a significant blood pressure drop that I hope will also contribute to the well-being of my brain.

But some conditions are not within one's power to control, such as the cancerous tumor in Jackie's breast that was revealed in late December by a mammogram, ultrasound, and biopsy. Two hours after a lumpectomy and biopsy in early January revealed nothing adverse in her lymph nodes, albeit a need for five weeks of preventive radiation, Jackie was dressed, ready to go home, and with typical self-reliance told her nurse she could walk with me to the parking lot. But she was prevented from doing so by hospital protocol. The next few days, Jackie continued her swift recovery without post-operative pain, and when the pain arrived a week after surgery, she took only a few of the prescribed hydrocodone pills. Why did she stop? "A person just has to live with this, has to accept it as part of who you are. Your body, after all, is part of who you are, so you just can't expect a prescription to heal all your problems, especially if it dulls your sensations." A truth she discovered from her bout with sciatica and that she had the strength to abide by.

After coming home with me so I could take care of her for a few days, Jackie prodded me to get the house ready for her longtime cleaningwoman, Lorena, and her crew. I spent the next week decluttering and relocating stuff I'd stashed away in the corners of several rooms. Books, medical reports, financial records, manuscripts, correspondence, and Christmas cards of yore. Every item a question. Ditch it or save it? Which resulted in a day of shelving books downstairs. Then another day sorting and relocating my papers in the file box that Jackie gave me a few years ago. Then at last a few days dusting and vacuuming, washing the bathroom and kitchen floors, cleaning the sinks and toilets, and polishing water fixtures. I was proud of having done a thorough job of cleaning the place, until Jackie told me "Now you've got it clean enough to be cleaned by Lorena."

The next day, when Lorena came to inspect the place in advance of cleaning it the following week, I gave her a complete tour, room by room, to which she responded with courteous smiles, but without any comments, either about the house or its appearance. In the upstairs bathroom, though, she stopped to look at a faint white line of mineral deposit around the base of the brass faucet where it adjoins the granite surface, which I took to be an incriminating detail. I wondered what else she'd been noting along the way. A week later after Lorena and her crew had spent four hours doing their stuff, woodwork throughout the house was so much cleaner and glowing that I had an embarrassing awareness of how many other things I must have overlooked in the course of my housecleaning. Which makes me wonder how many other things I've failed to notice the past six months.

Despite my failing perceptions, some things are impossible to overlook, especially in a chronicle about deep old age. Like the recent demise of a dear colleague, four years older than I, who died of a heart attack while cooking dinner for himself and his wife, whose dementia left her incapable of calling for help. It was a few days before their children discovered his body on the kitchen floor and her desperate helplessness, a horrific and pathetic story that compelled Jackie and me to realize we've not done anything to anticipate or deal with such a dreadful possibility. As if both of us believe we might be fortunate enough to go gently into that good night, without any trouble to ourselves or anyone else. Recently, though, Jackie suggested that we make arrangements to deal with such an event, so I proposed that we look into medical alert systems, but she went silent and then seemed to demur. At present, then, both of us are more aware than before, thanks to the calamity of others. But we've not yet taken heed (or action) like we did in advance of the polar vortex that descended on the Midwest in late January, with heavy snow, more than a foot in some places, and the coldest temperatures in more than twenty years, wind chills in some places of minus-seventy degrees. Severe weather, indeed, but not so daunting as the ultimate chill.

Eighty-Six to Eighty-Seven ⚶
Diet, Euthanasia, Aging Friends

MARCH 2019 TO AUGUST 2019

Thanks to the low-carb diet I started in December and continue to follow, I've reduced my waistline from thirty-eight to thirty-five inches, lowered my blood pressure (now 120s–130s over 60s–70s), and completely eliminated the painful epigastric hernia episodes of recent years. So, I feel much better and younger than before, as if I were in my mid seventies rather than late eighties. My sense of well-being was confirmed by my cardiologist a few weeks ago, when she congratulated me for having the lowest blood pressure of anybody she'd seen that day, and was also upbeat after checking my legs, ankles, heart, and lungs: "You're doing so well, there's nothing I can do for you. Thank you. You've made my day." At which point I knocked on wood to prevent her exuberance and mine from bringing bad luck. Despite that cautionary knock, her thank-you led me to believe my dietary regimen might be a source of universal well-being in old age—or any age.

That heady notion collapsed when I thought of Jackie, who weighs sixty pounds less than I, but almost always eats more than I, who doesn't skimp on the carbs and enjoys more wine, yet is more energetic, quick-witted, and free of health problems than I. So much for my dietary panacea. Though radiation therapy in January left her fatigued in February and early March, Jackie felt well enough in late March to visit Dick and Phyllis, our snowbird friends in Palm Springs, while I stayed home due to the increasing discomfort and hassles of flying. Since her return, she's felt so well and rested that a twenty-minute rest in late afternoon is enough to keep her zesty until bedtime at ten. In other words, both of us have enjoyed a reversal of our health problems the past six months.

In early April, we were buoyed by dinner and drinks at Bill's house, then by the three of us octogenarians trying to imagine what life might be like fifty or sixty years from now by remembering how much has evolved over the course of our lives. So, we talked of computers, the internet, smartphones, miniaturization, and self-driving automobiles, all of which led me to imagine the futuristic possibility of our being transported from one place in the world to another in an instant. But after explaining the impossibility of such a thing, Bill conceived the more plausible possibility of our being virtually transported to other places by high-tech multidimensional creations that will induce us to *believe* and *feel* that we are in those places. Given my yearning for another visit to Hawaii, where I haven't vacationed the past twelve years, I found the idea of a visit without the hassles of flying exhilarating. But I soon realized that Bill was envisioning a souped-up version of 3D films, which according to Wikipedia "have existed in some form since 1915," a thought that made me realize how difficult it is to transcend the limits of our past experience. How difficult as well to transcend the limits of our bodies, as we were reminded by the sight of Bill's gaunt and aged tiger cat, so robust a year ago.

A few days later, the visit of a longtime friend also reminded me of what could be in store for our aging bodies. He stopped in after taking his wife to work and told me of how her behavior had changed the past two years, drastic and unalterable changes that have burdened him in many ways—from driving her to and from work, to cooking and caring for her at home, and intervening on her behalf with her employer and others. No wonder he became agitated in telling me about her situation and his. A reminder of how things can change in ways that are irreversible, a disturbing possibility that made me wonder what I would do if Jackie became so disabled.

When I told her of that concern, Jackie said, "Both of my daughters know, and you know, I don't want to go on living if I'm mentally gone, can't take care of myself, and can't make my wishes known." Then she reminded me of the "do not resuscitate" directive that each of us signed and submitted to the University of Iowa Hospital last year. "But that form," I told her, "will only apply if you're a patient at that hospital facing a life-threatening condition. What if you're not in a hospital for any medical problem?" She quickly replied, "I want to be given an overdose of morphine like my mother got when she was in hospice." Which led me to ask her, "But what if you're mentally gone but not in a hospital or hospice and not suffering from a terminal illness or any serious medical problem?"

That question stymied both of us, given that terminal illness is a precondition of euthanasia in all the states where it's legally available to residents of the state. I made a Google search for sources of knowledgeable and experienced suicidal assistance, which led me to realize how few alternatives there are, each quite difficult to find: (1) a reliable doctor, such as Kevorkian in years past, who is willing to provide guidance or illegal assistance; (2) an active advocacy group, such as CompassionandChoices.org and DeathwithDignity.org, from which one can obtain reliable guidance or information; (3) an experienced, underground specialist, such as John Hofsess, a Canadian citizen, who assisted eight people who committed suicide between 1999 and 2001, and in 2016 flew to Switzerland where he was able to get legal assistance with his own suicide. After gathering that information, I told Jackie about it, and she said quite calmly, "I don't want to talk about this stuff anymore." So, I said no more. But I can't help thinking the pleasure of our present lives is predicated on a baseless hope of avoiding some kind of dementia, much as the pleasure of continuing to live in our comfortable homes is predicated on the tenuous hope that we'll never need assisted living.

A few days later, I discovered another foolish hope, when I took my twenty-year-old Jeep in for an oil change and check of its rusting underside. I assumed it would survive as long as I'm able to drive, until Alex, service manager at the local Jeep agency, showed me iPhone shots of holes in its chassis and warned, "They're a sign you're heading toward a nasty collapse on the passenger side." Visible rust on the rocker-panels had roused my concern about the chassis, and led me to read Jonathan Waldman's *Rust: The Longest War*, which details the destructive power of rust in cars, planes, ships, and the Statue of Liberty's interior steel frame. The news of those holes wasn't surprising, but the size of them and Alex's warning left me shaken, given the risk on Jackie's side of the car. Aging and rust—counterparts I never recognized before.

Driving home in my newly serviced Jeep, its engine and steering still in good shape, I was saddened by the prospect of having to part with it after so many years of trouble-free travel, first with Kate, then with Jackie. But no time for mourning, given the need to find an affordable replacement on the used-car market, ASAP. Two days later, thanks to an internet search on Cargurus.com, I found a 2007 Jeep Grand Cherokee eight miles away, eleven years younger than my old one, its stone-gray body aglow, its interior like new, its eight-cylinder engine more powerful than my six-cylinder. So advantageous in every respect that Jackie and I are still surprised by how little it cost—$4,300 plus the trade-in of my old Jeep. And I'm surprised by how swiftly my long-time attachment to that trusty car gave way to the attractions of its replacement. Better safe than sorry, a truth that also recently guided Hannah and Monty to leave their longtime home in Davis, California, and move to Whidbey Island in the Puget Sound, when California's fire-ridden air threatened her long-compromised lungs and potentially her life.

Lacking such an immediate danger, I continue to be so attached to my 120-year-old home that I cannot imagine leaving it.

Having lived, loved, cooked, dined, and written in it for forty-nine years, gardened on its back lot all those years, and witnessed the maturation of its surrounding trees, I consider it the oldest and one of the most influential attachments of my life. An outlandish love affair, of course, given the tightrope of continuing to live in a place so ill suited to someone my age. But I'm guided, at last, by the wisdom of Pascal that "the heart has its reasons that reason cannot know."

Speaking of the heart's reasons, when Jackie learned of the lump in her breast and the need to have it biopsied in December, she was roused by a bucket-list desire to see Mount Rushmore that led us to take a mid May road trip with our friends Pat and Stan, to see not only Mount Rushmore, but also some other historic places, all quite striking. On the way to Rushmore, we visited Frank Lloyd Wright's modernist Park Inn in Mason City, Iowa, then admired the celebratory grain-facade of the Corn Palace in Mitchell, South Dakota, followed by a tour of the survivalist hillside sod house of the Prairie Homestead in Philip, South Dakota, followed by a drive through the barren but exceptionally fascinating hills and hillocks of the Badlands National Park, inhabited by an invisible host of wild animals. Then, at last, Mount Rushmore, which welcomed us with such a windy rainstorm, we had only a brief glimpse of it before a swift drive home.

Back in Iowa City, I planted a handful of tomato seedlings in early June. A small fraction of past summer gardens, but even with the help of Dennis, my seventy-seven-year-old gardening assistant, who stood on a ladder and pounded in the seven-foot supporting stakes, I had so much trouble digging each hole, then kneeling and holding each plant in place while backfilling and watering, that in the midst of moving my unstable knees from one spot to the next I was suddenly moved to say, "It looks like this is endgame, Dennis. This is the last time I'll ever be able to do this routine, even with your help." A smile crossed his face, and I smiled too at the prospect of being done with all the bending over, kneeling, digging, and transplanting for which I'm now unfit. Yet

I was also deeply saddened by the end of a sixty-five-year passion for vegetable gardening, a passion that livened my days from March through November, from seed-time to harvest; that kept me in touch with the soil, the sun, the spring rains, the summer heat; and that inspired me to write *My Vegetable Love: A Journal of a Growing Season* and *Weathering Winter: A Gardener's Daybook.*

In late June, I was shocked by the death of my friend and former graduate student, Ned, an admirable essayist, dedicated scholar, and incomparable collaborator. Ned's zest for life, irrepressible good will, and wide-ranging public causes made me think he was unstoppable, until he emailed me in late March with news that his bladder cancer had returned and spread. Even after that I thought Ned would pull through, especially when he called in early June and told me of how the chemotherapy had made him eligible for immune therapy. But the chemo left him susceptible to infection, which did him in after a trip to New York City. A chill reminder of Didion's truth that "life changes in an instant."

I escaped such somber thoughts—and the July heat—by retreating indoors, reading and reading—from fantasy to actuality: from *Alice's Adventures in Wonderland* and *Through the Looking Glass* to Edna O'Brien's *The Love Object* and Frans de Waal's *Mama's Last Hug*, a compelling revelation of the many ways in which other creatures are akin to human beings in their mental and social behavior. And closer to home, Louise Aronson's *Elderhood: Redefining Aging, Transforming Medicine, Reimagining Life*, which embodies a profound reconception not only of elderly life and health problems, but also of appropriate care and medical treatment for the unique nature and risks of elderly illness, a work that has led me to be even more grateful for the cautious, low-risk care that Jackie and I have received from our internist.

My reading also included a batch of review essays about research on various methods of increasing longevity, such as transfusions of youthful blood, cell-nurturing supplements, disease-curing drugs, gene-based interventions, counterclockwise mental activities, brain-challenging computer games, and socio-stimulating projects. All are born of a widespread human desire to live longer and longer, healthier and healthier, feeling younger and younger, happier and happier, world without end. The irrepressible fantasy.

Though billions of dollars have been devoted to such research and development programs at corporate and university labs throughout the country, panaceas are not in the offing, as one can see from the most informative and thoughtful essays about life-extending/life-enhancing projects: Gregg Easterbrook's "What Happens When We All Live to 100?" (*The Atlantic*, October 2014); Tad Friend's "The God Pill" (*The New Yorker*, April 3, 2017); Adam Gopnik's "Can We Live Longer but Stay Younger?" (*The New Yorker*, May 20, 2019); and Bruce Grierson's "The Thought that Counts" (*The New York Times Magazine*, October 26, 2014). Given the wisdom of such essays, I'm grateful to have lived twenty-six years longer than average for a male of my generation, so I don't do anything special to increase my good fortune, beyond following the basic advice to sleep seven to eight hours a night, maintain a moderate diet and normal weight, exercise daily (physically and mentally), and enjoy sociable activity with Jackie and friends.

Fascinating as it was to read about widespread life-extending and life-enhancing research, it was more compelling to spend time with friends in their eighties and beyond who continue to make a difference, as if there were no such thing as retirement. Like Janet, now ninety-two, lively as always during a lunch at Oaknoll, where Jackie and I enjoyed her incisive wit. A former English professor and irrepressible teacher who has frequently offered novel-reading courses at the local senior-center, Janet has also been writing exquisite memory pieces, several of which she shared with me this year. Though she lives and dines at Oaknoll, Janet still shops for homegrown produce at the farmer's market, where I saw her a few weeks ago. She's her own person and has always been so, ever since we met fifty years ago.

The same is true of my former cardiologist, Allyn, whom I met twenty-three years ago. Now eighty-four and retired from the university's medical college after a distinguished career, he lives both in Iowa City and New York City, shuttling back and forth as if doing so were no more demanding than a drive to the airport twenty miles away. Why New York City? Because he's a cultural omnivore, captivated by the exceptional music and theatrical offerings of the city, as Jackie and I discovered during a dinner out in mid July, when he told us about some of his recent comings and goings. Yet he continues to be so devoted to the field of cardiology that for several years he's been at work on a book about pioneers of modern and contemporary heart care, as I discovered when he sent me a few chapters for reactions and suggestions.

Given my thirty-five years of heart problems, I had an immediate interest in his work, for I assumed it would shed light on origins of the life-saving diagnostic method and bypass surgery I received after my first heart attack in 1985, and it certainly did. What I didn't expect is that Allyn would reveal the personal side of all the doctors he writes about, even to the point of detailing their eccentricities. So, his work is at once medically significant and biographically compelling. A genuinely humanistic project.

In July, it was Gretchen who surprised us with an invitation to stop by for a late afternoon drink. Her face was marked by grief, but not a hint of self-pity or tears, though her husband, Howard, had died less than two weeks before. So attached to each other as to seem like one, they moved back and forth between their home in Iowa City and their retreat on the Spanish island of Ibiza. Several years ago, Jackie bought from Gretchen a painting of two identical birds, one feeding, the other attentively standing by its side, as in a still-life, like her and Howard. I was especially touched by Gretchen's account of his last weeks in the hospital and in hospice, both of them aware even before then of his impending demise from congestive heart failure. And it was fascinating to learn of how she'd grown up in a small town near Philadelphia, lived in New York City, sought a different landscape and life at the University of Colorado, then at the Academy of Fine Arts in Vienna, then with Howard in Ibiza. An exceptional artist, widely exhibited in the United States, Italy, and Spain, she continues to paint, but without thought of another show because, as she nodded in agreement, she's "not free not to paint."

A few days after our visit with Gretchen, Jackie and I took a walk in the cemetery near my house, the border of which led us to the graves of four former colleagues, two of whom hadn't been there the last time I visited, even though they had died several years before—all four tombstones standing next to each other, as if their residents might have been chatting in the main office or hallway of our department building. Likewise, several rows up was the tombstone of the department chair who hired me, and whose desk faced the department office so he could look out at us when we gathered to chat. This academic enclave was so much a part of my life in years past that I momentarily thought of rejoining its replica here in the cemetery when my time comes. But then I reaffirmed the decision to have my ashes scattered on the north shore of Kauai, where I scattered Kate's, where I often vacationed with her, then with Jackie, and where my daughters still visit. In the long run, of course, no one will care about the whereabouts of my ashes. In the short run, though, I hope Jackie and my children enjoy that beguiling half-moon bay and the satisfaction of scattering my ashes and their leis in its waters. On the other hand, I also understand why Jackie has chosen as her final resting place an anonymous commemorative spot that contains the ashes of those whose bodies are dissected by University of Iowa medical students.

In the wake of such musings, it was a pleasure to behold my son Marshall when he arrived at the airport, now sixty-two but looking much more fit and muscular than I did at his age, thanks to his morning runs and other exercises—but thankfully no longer doing marathons and half-marathons. It is also a pleasure to hear him reminisce about his childhood and adolescent days here in Iowa City—so vividly I was in awe of his detailed memory of things. And touched by his wistful remark that "this is the only childhood home I can still return to," which put me in mind of a remark that Kate made forty-nine years ago, when we bought the house—"I hope this will be a place that's always home for your children." No wonder he took it upon himself to sand and clean the six-foot, round redwood table when I told him we were having a potluck dinner on the terrace a few days after he arrived—and before leaving, he spent a couple of hours tending and turning things in my three-bin composter. I never imagined myself living long enough to have children so mature, thoughtful, and generous as he.

A couple of days after he flew home in mid August, Jackie and I had another memorable day on Lake Macbride with our friend Sharon, who motored us from one leg of it to the other at a gentle and quiet pace, as she did last year. Again past the inlets where Marshall and I spent early mornings wetting our lines and bringing a few fish home for dinner. Now, like Sharon, I've given up fishing because as she agreed "their life is all they have," and "it's hard to do catch and release without damaging them." But it sure was a pleasure to go once more to that captivating lake, where we stopped awhile near shore to savor Jackie's chicken, orzo, and green bean salad while chatting about the ambitious showplace homes being built where more intimate and amiable cabins like Sharon's once stood. The more things change, alas, the more things change. But I'd much rather be on that lake with Jackie and Sharon than meditating on "transcendentally important things," as advised in a solemn piece about aging I recently read. Instead of contemplating transcendental things, Jackie and I are devoted to the here and now. So, we're heading up to a cabin on Lake Superior. "Seize the day" is our mantra.

Eighty-Seven ✹

Final Wishes, Last Cuz, Having a Life

AUGUST 2019 TO FEBRUARY 2020

How strange to realize that in seven years of working on this chronicle I've said little about the disposal of my remains except for a few sentences about having my ashes scattered on the north shore of Kauai. Come to think of it, why haven't I written Jackie and my children about it, so they'll know what to do when the time comes? Not because of a reluctance to trouble them with a foreboding of it, so much as a carelessness about putting important matters in writing. For example, eighteen years ago I bought insurance policies for Kate and myself at a local funeral business to cover the costs of cremation and of shipping our bodies back to Iowa City if need be. Given that Kate was ten years younger, I assumed she would outlive me and notify the funeral company of my death. Also, that she would scatter my ashes on the north shore of Kauai, where I had promised to scatter hers. But after her death, I forgot to write my children about the insurance policy and its whereabouts, as well as about cremation at the local funeral business. Come to think of it, I should have written them when I bought both policies, in the event that Kate and I died simultaneously. Given their longtime awareness that I wanted my ashes scattered on Kauai, I should also have written them about my recent decision to have the ashes scattered around a tree in Reno Street Park, two houses away from where I've lived for almost fifty years.

But why am I fretting about these matters right now? Because I just finished reading Elizabeth Thomas's no-nonsense book, *Growing Old: Notes on Aging with Something Like Grace*. Near the end of it she declares that "your loved ones don't want to think about your death and may not be prepared," so it's essential to write a document stating your "preferences," in order that they "know what to do when the time comes." She recommends posting it "on the refrigerator or perhaps on the kitchen wall," where "everyone will see it." Instead I've emailed the following letter about my preferences to Jackie and my children, with copies to my attorney, the local funeral business, and my internist at University of Iowa Hospital, so everyone will know my final wishes when the time comes.

Dear Jackie, Hannah, Marshall, and Amy,

Though I've long wanted my ashes scattered on the north shore of Kauai, I now prefer a spot close to where I've lived, loved, and gardened for almost fifty years. Specifically, I'd like my ashes scattered under a tulip tree that I donated to Reno Street Park several years ago. It's a stone's throw from 416 Reno Street, a place filled with memories for all of us. The tree is near the northeast corner of the lot, easily identifiable in spring, summer, and fall by its tulip-shaped leaves.

Note: I have made arrangements for cremation at Lensing's, a local funeral business, where I purchased an insurance policy eighteen years ago to cover the costs of cremation and of shipping my body back to Lensing's if need be.

As for other doings, I do not want a funeral service of any kind or any religion. If anyone wishes to plan a memorial service, my only request is that there be no religion or religious activities connected with it. Most of all, I'd be delighted by a joyous get-together with food and drinks at 416 Reno Street (if possible).

With all my love for all the years to come.

February 15, 2020

Speaking of memorial services, a late October tribute to Ned, who died last June, brought several of us together at Prairie Lights bookstore—mostly his longtime friends from graduate school, now scattered throughout the country. Jackie and I hosted a pre-reading get-together at my place. Though it was a pleasure to see all of them again, more than twenty-five years after graduate school, their collective presence heightened my sense of his absence, as did their eloquent and humorous tributes. In the process of delivering my tribute, I also remembered another reading I gave several years ago at Prairie Lights, a joint reading with Ned from our collaborative work, *Essayists on the Essay*. Which made me even more aware of his absence. Reminders never end.

A week later, in early November, I had a quite different experience of presence and absence, thanks to an email from my cousin Howard, the last paternal relative of my generation: "Just a brief question CUZ. Are you still on this earth?" Such a spare and surprising question, out of the blue, after nothing from him the past two years, I wondered whether it was motivated by cousinly interest in my well-being or by a competitive impulse—i.e., which of us (both eighty-seven, born two months apart) will outlast the other. I responded with a genial interest in his situation and account of my own: "Yes, cuz, I'm still here, and delighted to see that you are too. I'm still doing the treadmill four or five days a week, still writing, still taking all my meds, and still enjoying my days aboveground. I hope all is well with you and your loved ones." I assumed he would send me a reply. But his continued silence almost three months later, when I started writing this piece, made me wonder if he's "still on this earth" or if he was only interested in my no longer being on it, and perhaps disappointed by my reply. I wondered, in other words, if the proximity of our births and our old age had engendered a competitive impulse—as in a marathon. For I can hardly deny that my genial response was also competitive. An endgame of sorts, quite different from the Monopoly games of our teenage years.

A few days ago, Howard surprised me again, this time with a phone call, and we reminisced like long-lost friends, dear cousins still on this earth, catching up on so many things about each other. It was a reunion beyond compare, capped by the promise that I'd send him a copy of this paragraph which roused his laughter as I read it to him over the phone. But when I asked Howard about his wife, Eileen, the laughter suddenly stopped, and he told me, "she died of cancer three months ago and I can't talk about it." I was stunned by the news, and then realized why he'd not been in touch the past two years and why he sent me that brief query three months ago about being on this earth, just a week before she died. Not competing but reaching out in the face of profound loss.

Three months ago, at the time of Howard's query and my reply, I was feeling quite well. But the past several months I've been troubled by brief but painful hernia episodes that made me worry about the possibility of others in the months to come. Having had ten months without an episode, thanks to my weight-loss regimen, I was surprised by the first one in late November. After the second one in late December, I started wearing a hernia belt to keep it in place during treadmill exercise or while standing and cooking dinner, and in hope of avoiding corrective surgery. After the most recent episode in late January, my internist called the university's hernia clinic for a consult about the benefits and risks of surgical repair, and the two surgeons who examined me agreed with my preference to keep it controlled with the hernia belt. So, I'm grateful for that reprieve.

I'm also pleased by my cardiologist's upbeat heart exam early in February, based on an echocardiogram indicating that it pumps in the same near-normal to normal range as two years ago. Icing the cake, her accompanying intern told me, "You look much younger than your age, like seventy-five rather than eighty-seven."

Most of the time, I also feel quite good, thanks to the weight loss, an increased water intake of five cups a day, a bodily sense of well-being, an ease in getting around—and my heart-healthy avoidance of articles and news programs about the doings of Donald Trump.

I'm also feeling upbeat, thanks to the realization of how intangibles such as mood, attitude, outlook, resilience, and experience can enlighten and enrich one's later years—as I learned from recent books on advanced age, such as Aronson's *Elderhood* and Thomas's *Growing Old*, as well as from Don, a retired professor of psychology, whose wisdom has helped me think about my current life in a more affirmative way than before. During a recent after-dinner conversation with Don, I told him about the return flight from my granddaughter Lizzie's wedding in California, eighteen months ago, which left me with such swollen legs for several days that I've not taken a plane ever since. Having grounded myself, it seemed like I'd shrunk my life in order to save it, or at least to reduce potential threats to it, a trade-off that left me wondering whether I had paid too high a price for such insurance. The minute I expressed those concerns, Don flashed a smile and told me, "but you have a life." A surprising response from someone who has long had the status of a 100,000-mile-a-year air traveler.

At first, I thought his assertion that I have a life meant he was implying that life itself is to be prized, even if it doesn't include air travel. In other words, that a shrunken life is better than having none at all, which could result from a stroke or heart attack in the midst of a flight, given my history of Afib, heart disease, and heart failure. A compelling reminder that led me to thank him for his sensible point of view. Later that evening, I realized the idiomatic gist of Don's assertion and its profound implications not only about having a life that transcends mere existence, but also about accepting and enjoying the scope of it and the trade-offs, whatever they happen to be. Like my new dairy-free, low protein diet that led me to find an online recipe for wild rice soup without any meat or dairy, comprised of vegetable broth, wild rice, sautéed onions, celery, and mushrooms, flavored with dry sherry, curry powder, and a dab of Dijon mustard, thickened slightly with a bit of flour. The resulting soup was so zingy that when Jackie had a taste of it, she asked me to make a pot of it for our next dinner together.

That soup epitomizes a realistic and informative way of thinking about life in one's eighties that Aronson, Thomas, and others expound in their books about advanced age. Their books, together with Don's wisdom, have led me to see that despite all my chronic medical problems, dietary restrictions, and relinquished activities like air travel and gardening, I do indeed have a life, one more abundant than I had previously imagined. Being in love with Jackie. Being visited by Amy, Hannah, and Marshall. Being in touch with my granddaughters Kathleen and Lizzie, who've recently told me about great-grandchildren on the way, and with my granddaughter Micaela, who sends me news and pictures of my first great-grandchild, Olivia. Being advised by my grandson, Owen, about the ins and outs of TV technology and cable services. And being entertained by the pleasures of reading, writing, cooking, and socializing.

Thanks also to vivid documentaries, I've traveled to the Arctic and the tropics, beheld mountainous and underwater life. Thanks as well to captions, which compensate for my severe hearing loss, I've enjoyed a wide range of outstanding movies, especially during the run-up to this year's Oscars—movies as varied and striking as *1917*, *A Beautiful Day in the Neighborhood*, *American Factory*, *Judy*, *Marriage Story*, *Once Upon a Time in Hollywood*, *One Child Nation*, *Parasite*, and *The Two Popes*.

Jackie's hearing, by contrast, is still so good that she's able to enjoy the full range of live performances—from lectures, readings, and vocal concerts to play productions and musicals—which she attends with her longtime friends. Though I sometimes wish my hearing were good enough to enjoy such events, I don't have the stamina for a social life as varied and active as hers. Given that she still has no chronic ailments, Jackie has the get-up-and-go for a full menu of movies, concerts, plays, and musicals, as well as for days filled with all sorts of doings that might include a strenuous exercise session with her trainer, shopping at Trader Joe's, lunching or dining with friends and acquaintances, helping the needy, occasionally counseling home-hunters, talking at length with high-tech service consultants for one or another of her malfunctioning high-tech gadgets or services, and so on. A purposeful and enjoyable life, especially for an eighty-four-year-old.

The only problem is that advanced age periodically takes her by surprise and suddenly she's beset with a midafternoon collapse. Reviewing my notes of the past six months, such episodes occurred every two or three weeks, followed by an earnest vow to cut back on her activities, followed by so speedy a bounce-back, thanks to her resilience, that it's easy to see how she's then swept up in another round of captivating activities. She has an appetite for life beyond compare that I beheld just a few days ago, when a collapse on Tuesday afternoon, marked by an anguished phone call, was followed by a day of rest, then dinner out on Wednesday with me and a couple of friends—so vivacious it seemed like she was sixty-four rather than eighty-four. With years more to go.

But whenever I think that she and I have years to go, I'm chastened by memories of our friend Joe, so vigorous in so many ways that I ended a previous installment with a celebratory paragraph about him as "a manifold artist, undaunted by age." Early this November, however, when we visited Joe and his wife Genie, he was on the verge of death: on a reclining chair under a blanket, his head on a pillow, eyes closed as if asleep, thanks to a painrelieving opiate. Joe's Oaxacan streetscapes at each end of the room reminded me of his second home and perennial visits there. Reminded me too of how energetic he'd been while sketching portraits of Jackie and me in pencil, ink, and pastel, conversing with us nonstop about painting, music, and his love of choral singing, so energetic and gifted that I was moved to write that earlier sketch of him. Now so quiet I was at a loss for words, but Jackie broke the silence and brightened the mood by telling Genie about the landscapes and portraits of Rose Franzen, an Iowa artist whose work we'd seen at a museum the day before, then asking Genie if she knew about Franzen. A question that Joe answered with a "yes" and then went silent again until he gave another "yes" to one of Jackie's later questions. Each "yes" was a surprise, given Joe's prior silence and his head turned away from us. But Jackie set me straight later on when she said, "No matter how weak and out of it one might seem, the hunger to be part of things persists to the very end." A truth worth heeding to the very end.

In late February, I received another reminder of how swiftly one's fate can change, when my oncologist told me that the non-Hodgkin's lymphoma he diagnosed five years ago is no longer quiescent. Thus, he prescribed four immunotherapy infusions during March, one a week, of a medication named Rituxan that will impair my immune system and possibly cause other unpleasant side effects. Like Philip Roth, I wonder "how long my luck holds out." Long enough, I hope, to tell about my late eighties in the midst of a worrisome treatment for a suddenly worrisome lymphoma.

Eighty-Seven to Eighty-Eight 🖋
Cancer, Covid, Protests, Cannoli

In early March, a week before the start of immunotherapy, Marshall flew in for a few days to raise my spirits and help me prepare for the coronavirus. Though it didn't seem imminent in Iowa, he thought I should get some antibacterial disinfectants in advance. And he was spot on, for Purell products were sold out, and Wet Ones the only high-quality hand wipes in town. I hadn't expected widespread stockpiling, but the panic was evidently well under way, as infectious as the virus.

Though not panicked by the virus, I was worried about Rituxan, the immunotherapy drug, especially after visiting its website and discovering it "can cause serious side effects that can lead to death." When I told Jackie about that warning, she chided me for fretting about it: "Do you think the distinguished oncologist who saved your life ten years ago would endanger it now?" A thoughtful question that left me puzzled until a doctor at University of Iowa Hospital set me straight—"even when reactions are rare, even less than one percent, drug manufacturers make those warnings to protect themselves from lawsuits."

Despite that knowledgeable explanation, a few days later I panicked about being undone by Rituxan and wrote a new will without legal consultation, updating all my bequests in time to have it notarized before the first infusion. Then I breathed a sigh of relief, then wondered why I had waited twelve years to revise my 2008 will in such a whirlwind. The child of panic is folly. The next morning, I went to the infusion center playing mind games to put myself at ease. I chatted up Stacey the nurse, to conceal my anxiety when she gave me three pills to reduce side effects, which made me even more worried about impending side effects. After a couple of hours without any discomfort, I was delighted by Stacey's estimate that the infusion would be finished in a few hours rather than seven. During the last two hours I was on cloud nine, reading and savoring the tuna-fish salad I packed for lunch. Would I have been ecstatic had I not been panicked?

The second infusion, a week later, turned out to be as trouble-free as the first, and speedier too. So, I calmed down and turned my attention to the virus, for the first case of it in Iowa had been discovered in Iowa City, and the risk of it multiplying without social distancing led the university, like others throughout the country, to plan on using a combination of classroom and online teaching next fall. A worrisome prospect that made me apprehensive about the prospect of changes in every kind of interpersonal activity.

My first experience of the changes took place a few days later when I had an appointment with my oncologist, but had to pass a security check by masked medical assistants before entering the hospital. And when I met with my oncologist, he was equipped not only with a mask but also a large plastic face shield. When I asked if he envisioned additional therapy in late spring or early summer, he said, "It'll depend on the benefits and the risks." And when I asked about the risks, he said, "The risk of bringing you into the hospital." A catch-22 indeed—being infected by the virus while being in the hospital for immunotherapy. But it didn't upset me like the Rituxan website, because the virus at that point didn't seem like an immediate threat.

The next day, though, I got a wake-up call when our friend Cheryl turned up at my back door, a big smile on her face, to pick up some tomato seeds I'd forgotten to put on the outside bench the night before. After retrieving them from the fridge, I opened the back door, packets in hand, pushed open the storm door, and she instantly backpedaled, her face panic-stricken, a swift and striking change that made me realize how blasé I'd become about the virus and thus how negligent of social distancing. Cheryl's panicked reaction also made me realize that Jackie and I had been too complacent about being together on the weekends and for occasional dinners at my place. So, I called Jackie, told her of my concerns, and we agreed to stay apart from each other as much as possible until the virus is past or a vaccine available. An imperative, given my infusion-compromised immune system and our advanced age, but a bizarre way to spend our few remaining years, at a distance from each other.

Jackie called several days later to tell me she was on her way to my place with some of her coffee cookies—an addiction of mine she loves to indulge. I put on my mask and went out to meet her as she came up the driveway. Before rolling down her window to give me the cookies, she put on her mask. Then we talked a few minutes and did our best to smile at each other through our masks. And then she was gone like a fleeting memory of life before the virus.

The remaining infusions were almost as trouble-free as before, except for an afternoon and evening of severe chills followed by a fever that produced a restless night, followed by another week of interrupted sleep, all of which left me quite weakened. So, I used all the well-known remedies to get a good night's sleep again and again and again. Which not only left me feeling more rested, but also more energetic, mentally alert, and keenly aware that sleep is fundamental to well-being.

While being apart, Jackie and I continued to keep up with each other two or three times a day, via email and cell phone, not only about our doings but also about movies and TV series we'd been streaming and books we'd been reading. During one of our conversations, she was very upbeat about being home alone, reading, working in her garden, and relaxing. Jackie was enjoying the solitude so much, she realized (perhaps for the first time) why I've been inclined that way during our years together, whereas she's always been on the go. But as the weeks went by with Jackie at a distance, I was increasingly less content with being isolated, and didn't find any solace in all the signs proclaiming "We're in this together."

The loss of Jackie's physical presence made me receptive to her suggestion that I get a companionable cat, especially after she emailed me a shot of one, a medium-gray tiger, together with rave remarks from its foster caretaker, and an appealing note of her own: "Think about having this friend sitting next to you." An attractive shot, congenial thought, and delicious name—Cannoli—which led Jackie and me to meet her at the city animal shelter, where we were charmed by her shy-friendly ways, hiding at one moment, coming to be petted the next. We were also intrigued by the facts of her life—a five-year-old stray, a foundling, with a limp from a prior injury of her left-front paw. A perfect companion for an octogenarian. Hoping to be a good companion to her, I asked about Cannoli's needs and likes, learned she enjoys playing now and then, but more often cuddling and napping. Given those preferences, I went home to get things ready for her arrival—cozy napping spots, a cushioned cat carrier/bed, and catnip toys. Jackie in turn was a lavish godmother and insisted not only on paying the adoption fee but also buying dry food, wet food, bone-aiding supplements, a scratch pad, litter box, and litter.

Bringing Cannoli home in early May was a very different prospect from the infusions of March, as if I'd been transported to an entirely different place, which made me realize I was taking Cannoli to a different place from the foster home where she reportedly had been very happy. Her wailing all the way home made me wonder how long it would take her to adapt to an octogenarian and his aged home, given such an incomprehensible change in her life.

As the lockdown wore on, Jackie also had problems adjusting

to changes in her life—"I don't know what is wrong with me. I am so darned tired every afternoon. Or maybe I am 'sick' and don't know it. I have not been feeling myself for weeks." That troubling message and others like it made me think she should contact her internist, but I didn't say so, because Jackie has always been averse to bothering her doctors. I knew she wouldn't heed my advice. Jackie's further discussions of her problems helped me see that she was upset not just by social distancing and social isolation but also by worldwide suffering from the pandemic, by the horrors of Trump, by the deaths of longtime friends, and by physical inertia that left her feeling out of shape from lack of daily exercise. Problems largely beyond the expertise of an internist or the consolations of an absent loved one.

I wasn't any more helpful with Cannoli when I brought her home. As soon as I unzipped her cat carrier, she scurried into the kitchen, the living room, the dining room, under chairs, behind the couch and the plant stand, sniffing and eyeballing the perimeter of things. A frenzied tour, until she scooted under the corner cupboard in the dining room and hid for several hours, before bounding upstairs and hiding under a bed for several more. Her hectic and panicky arrival was unlike the behavior of any other cat I adopted the past sixty-five years. But then she calmly reappeared for a stop at her food and water bowls, as well as her litter box—the first signs of making herself at home.

The next day, after a few more hours in hiding, she suddenly reappeared, hopped up on the couch with me and was surprisingly companionable—cuddling and nuzzling as if we were dear friends. A prelude to more affectionate moments in the days that followed, which made me wonder if her years as a stray had been so rough and risky that she knew a good berth when she found it, much as my days of social isolation led me to know a good companion when I found her.

But Cannoli's captivating presence didn't distract me enough to dispel a growing fixation on the virus, roused every day since mid March by the need to be isolated in order to avoid it, and heightened every day by its prominence in newspapers and magazines, on the internet, radio and TV, all of which I consulted every day from then on. The compulsion to keep track of things intensified in late May, when most of the southern and southwestern states began relaxing their lockdowns, despite warnings that without prior evidence of declining infections and deaths, the virus would become more virulent. A dangerous disconnect between public policy and public well-being, the consequences of which I felt driven to follow in detail.

But in early May, I felt compelled once again to be concerned with the ongoing lymphoma, when my oncologist told me that because the Rituxan infusions had barely reduced the swelling in my groin, another series of infusions was in the offing with a more potent immunotherapy, together with another specialized drug. Without more therapy, he predicted the lymphoma would grow large enough to impinge on nearby organs and become life-threatening. I agreed to start the infusions in August, when this chronicle is completed and I've had more time to get rested up for the likelihood of unpleasant side-effects.

Getting a good night's sleep was complicated for several days by a problem with Cannoli, who turned out to be an eager bedtime companion. Indeed, after I went to bed one night, she managed to paw open her downstairs bathroom door, make her way through the darkened first floor, up the stairway to the second and into my bedroom; then hopped onto the bed and nudged me awake, as if she thought I might be game for some nighttime cuddling. But my previous sleep-loss episode made me unreceptive to being nudged or hopped on in bed. The next night I closed my door before she arrived, though I felt badly about rejecting her advances.

A few days later, my friend Duane sent me a video of monarch butterflies, thousands of them, companionably hibernating en masse in towering trees. All those butterflies together without bothering each other led me to think Cannoli and I could surely get on together without bothering each other. That night I kept my door open, and during the first few nights when she tried to wake me too early in the morning, I pushed her away several times, until she got the message a week later. Now she spends part of the evening on the bottom shelf of a pie safe in my bedroom, or on my bed or on a bed in the guest room across the hall, and bides her time in a window-lookout until I get up.

Working things out with Cannoli took place a few days before I turned eighty-eight, like an early birthday present. And the day itself was very happy, thanks to the companionship of Jackie whom I hadn't seen in more than two weeks, and to the sight of a blue sky after a week of rainy weather. She arrived with a marinated chicken breast and a homemade rhubarb pie—two of my favorites. Before we savored the goodies, Jackie took me for a ride by some attractive homes, as if she were in realtor mode again and I an out-of-town client. Back home, we roasted the chicken breast and enjoyed it with a crisp romaine salad, angel hair pasta, and sauvignon blanc, everything as delicious as the day itself, especially Jackie's tangy rhubarb pie with vanilla ice cream. Mindful of the virus, we dined at my outdoor picnic table, six feet apart from each other. A joyous eighty-eighth from start to finish.

A horrific day after, when I watched a white Minneapolis policeman pushing his knee and his weight down on the neck of a Black man, indifferent to the man's repeated plea, "I can't breathe, I can't breathe," indifferent to the man crying out for his mother, indifferent to bystanders' pleas to relent. And unchallenged by his three nearby cohorts, as impassive and expressionless as he, as if such a brutal murder was nothing out of the ordinary. Striking evidence not only of police brutality, but also of the relentless subjugation and suffering of Blacks in America.

No wonder the murder led to protests day and night for more than a month, spreading from Minneapolis to more than 2,000 cities and towns in all fifty states, as well as cities throughout the world. The largest and most widespread civil rights movement in history, much larger than the protests I remember from the 1960s, and much more diverse. Young and old, Black and white and Latinx, urging not only substantial reform of police depart-ments, but also a radical transformation in the perception, status, and treatment of Blacks in America and throughout the world. The protests roused so many aggressive police attempts to quell the upheaval that Jackie and I and millions of others were appalled by their blatant and widespread brutality. Especially by the spectacle of peaceful protesters dispelled from the White House grounds by low-flying military helicopters and D.C. po-lice firing rubber bullets and tear gas in order to clear a path for Trump to have a photo-op, Bible in hand, in front of a nearby church. The "law and order" president an epitome of lawless-ness, subsequently threatening to use attack dogs and military troops to subdue protesters. I have never been so disturbed by public events as I was by the police murder of George Floyd, and never so excited by public events as by the massive protests that followed and the promising signs of reform.

Mid June brought the best news of this spring, when my granddaughter Lizzie gave birth to a seven-pound, eight-ounce girl, Samantha Kay. What a pleasure to behold my second great-grandchild in a snapshot, sleeping peacefully in a sunflowery wrap with a big colorful bow above her forehead. Several weeks later, I received another shot of her, eyes wide open, a gentle smile, and her cheeks aglow, so at ease and pleased it made me eager to see the first shots of my next great-grandchild, coming in mid August when my granddaughter Kathleen gives birth. Joyous happenings I'd much rather write about (and think about) than the lymphoma in my left leg, left thigh, and groin, which swelled so much in mid June that I reported it to my oncologist, who started infusions again in late June, rather than August as previously planned.

I was also disturbed by the virus's resurgence throughout most of the southern and western states that had prematurely reopened for business in May and early June. The consequences predicted by epidemiologists made headlines in newspaper and TV reports, not only tallying the exceptional number of new cases in those states, but also highlighting the nationwide totals of more than

2,700,000 cases and 130,000 deaths as of early July—more than one quarter of the cases and deaths worldwide. An alarming statistic that makes me wonder if I'll live to see a virus-free or vaccine-cured country. Jackie feels the same way about her own uncertain future.

I have never been beset by such gloomy thoughts, not during the eight years of keeping this journal or anytime before, not even during heart attacks, bypass surgery, or stage 4 cancer. But I've never been at once so aged, beset with infirmities, and threatened by something like the virus. On the other hand, I've never been inclined to give up or give in, whatever the circumstances, especially not now with such beloved ones to live for as Jackie and Cannoli—and this chronicle to finish. Thus, I've been inspired by my oncologist's feisty remark when he examined me again—"We haven't even begun to fight."

The fight hadn't begun because one of the two drugs for the new therapy, Revlimid, was so fraught with dangerous side effects that I had to sign an affidavit acknowledging awareness of all its risks. Then I had to have a phone interview with a special CVS pharmacist to determine its compatibility with my medical history and other medications. Given those hassles and the drug's potential side effects, I had mixed feelings about taking the pills, especially after discovering their exorbitant cost.

In the midst of that unpleasant business, Jackie brought me a diverting newspaper article about black bears in Iowa, noting that "unlike cougars and wolves, bears have lips and a tongue that can be manipulated to pluck the smallest mulberry from a tree or extract a termite from a log." The article also contained surprising information about wildlife in Iowa before the Civil War—not only black bears but also bison, bobcats, coyotes, deer, elk, mountain lions, otters, wild turkeys, and wolves. In other words, not a farmscape, but a variegated landscape of prairies, wetlands, and forests, inhabited both by a wide range of animals and by native Americans, rather than settlers. A very different place from what it was like just seventy-five years later when I was born, which made me realize that industrial and technological developments during my lifetime are no more remarkable than the radical changes that took place in the wake of Euro-American settlement. No matter how long one lives, or how consequential it might seem, a lifetime is, after all, a fleeting moment in the flow of continuous change.

But life's brevity makes its unusual moments stand out more vividly, especially in old age, as I discovered after dinner on the Fourth of July, when Jackie surprised me by proposing that we get married. In years past, she wouldn't consider marriage, given how it would complicate each of our estate plans. But that concern was overriden by her worry that without being married we wouldn't have hospital visitation rights in the event of a medical crisis. For several weeks, then, we planned on getting married without giving up our separate homes, until I discovered that a federal regulation, proposed by Obama, negated the marriage requirement in cases of hospital visitation rights. Which led us to continue our sixteen-year love affair without the need to exchange any vows. Though I have recently learned that some hospitals might require a special Health Care Decisions document before granting visitation rights, I have not attempted to procure such a document, because I no longer travel anywhere and have already been assured visitation rights at the University of Iowa Hospital.

Now in mid summer, I am surprised at how much my view of the virus has changed from the beginning of this installment, when it seemed to be a distant matter, though it was already spreading throughout the U.S. Marshall and I were naïve enough to think antibacterial hand wipes and the like would be sufficient preparation for its arrival. I never imagined it would turn into a worldwide menace, upending the lives of billions, whether infected by it or not. Only the epidemiologists foresaw the possibility of such an outcome, and all too few in our country heeded their scientific guidance. No wonder case counts in the U.S. now exceed 5,000,000, and deaths total more than 175,000, statistics that might double or worse by the end of the year.

Though the virus is menacingly widespread, my home and solitary living arrangement have enabled me to avoid infection with relative ease. And this chronicle has been such an absorbing indoor project that social isolation has not been a costly or difficult imposition, as it certainly has for many others, such as the suddenly unemployed or those compelled to work from home with children to care for. On the other hand, I'm keenly aware of how the virus has circumscribed my life, distancing me from Jackie more often than not, cutting me off from the pleasures of being out and about with her and friends, doing things together, socializing in ways that cannot be matched by Zoom or other virtual get-together apps. But the deprivations are clearly offset by the necessity of social distancing to prevent infection by the virus. Indeed, I'm impressed by the many adjustments that people, agencies, and businesses have made to reduce exposure to it. And I'm grateful that social distancing led Jackie to urge that I adopt Cannoli, without whom I might be very touch-deprived.

When I first thought about this final installment in late February 2020, I did not imagine it would focus on such matters as I've discussed in the preceding paragraph—the pandemic, social isolation, distancing from Jackie, and the companionship of Cannoli. Nor did I expect to be writing about brutal police treatment of Blacks and the nationwide protests that ensued. Most of all, I expected to offer advice about the ninth decade based on personal experience. But in looking back over the eight years of this chronicle, I've come to realize that my longevity has in significant ways been a result of good luck, of fortunate circumstances, such as living just a mile and a half from exceptional medical care at the University of Iowa and of having low-cost health insurance thanks to being a retired professor. Even the knowledge of how and when to seek care for my numerous chronic conditions is in large part the result of good luck, thanks to having grown up in a family of doctors. Indeed, my longevity despite all those high-risk chronic conditions is probably a byproduct in part of genetic good luck. Given such good fortune, the only advice I can offer based on personal experience is to heed the words of one's doctors. But I'm intrigued by the advice of contemporary gurus and gerontologists who believe that lifespan is increased by an optimistic, caring, and joyous embrace of old age, assuming of course that one's condition in old age inclines one to embrace it. If so, "living longer" might well be "the happy problem of our time," as Lillian Hellman said in her old age.

I wonder, though, how to know and prepare for the time when longevity is a reason for gravity rather than levity. While I'm no longer deluded by my adolescent fantasy of immortality and I share Jackie's desire for the right to die if beset by terminal illness or dementia, there's still an indeterminate period of extended life that I'm presently enjoying, despite the ongoing lymphoma, and I'd like to enjoy it as long as possible. Which leads me to wonder how I'll know before it's time to let go. I wish there were well-known hargingers so I could take my leave before the trouble begins. But perhaps I should forget about harbingers and simply enjoy the time that's left. What will be, will be.

Acknowledgments ❧

I AM GRATEFUL TO the following people for their generous and valuable help: Jackie Blank, not only for her reactions and suggestions, but also for allowing me to write about her in extensive personal detail, without ever asking me to omit any of the details; Holly Carver for her overall editorial guidance, as well as for her thoughtful responses to draft sections and versions of the chronicle; and Michele Morano for taking time to provide reactions and suggestions while also chairing an English Department, raising a child, and working on her recent memoir.

Thank you to Charlotte Wright for her editorial expertise, to Sara Sauers for the elegant book design, and to Claudia McGehee for her beautiful cover art.

I am also grateful to the exceptional doctors and nurses who have helped me live long enough to produce this extended chronicle.